AUTHENTIC TRANSCRIPTIONS
WITH NOTES AND TABLATURE

BEST OF
THE WHO

Cover photo by Jeffrey Mayer

ISBN 0-634-02226-1

HAL•LEONARD®
CORPORATION

7777 W. BLUEMOUND RD. P.O. BOX 13819 MILWAUKEE, WI 53213

Visit Hal Leonard Online at
www.halleonard.com

BEST OF THE WHO

Athena

Words and Music by Peter Townshend

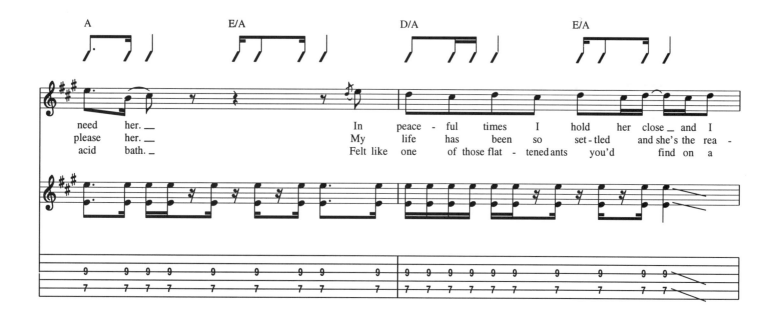

need her. ___
please her. ___
acid bath. ___

In peace - ful times I hold her close ___ and I
My life has been so set - tled and she's the rea -
Felt like one of those flat - tened ants you'd find on a

feed ___ her. ___
- son. ___
cra - zy path. ___

My heart starts pal - pi - tat - in' when I think my
Just one word from her ___ and my trou - bles are
I'd of topped my - self to give her time she did - n't

To Coda 1
End Rhy. Fig. 1A

guess was wrong. ___
long gone.
need to ask.

But I think I'll get a - long. ___
But I think I'll get a - long. ___
Was I a su - i - ci - dal psy - co - path?

She's just a

End Rhy. Fig. 1

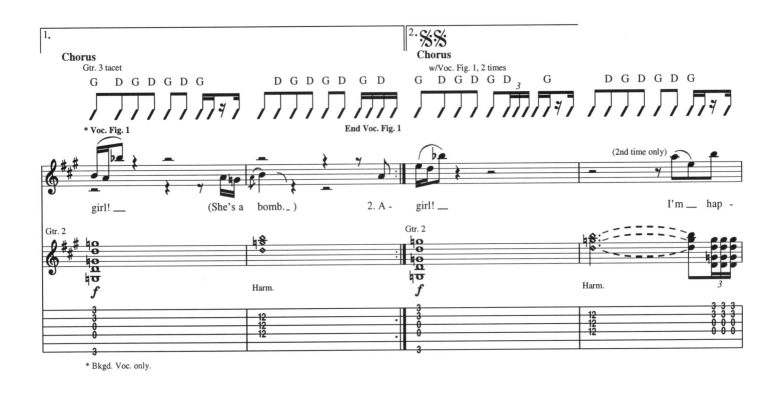

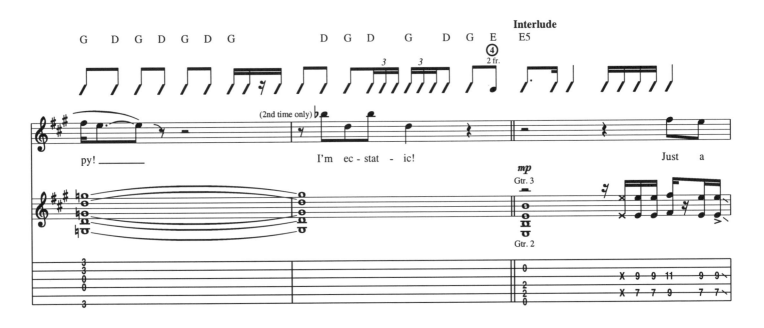

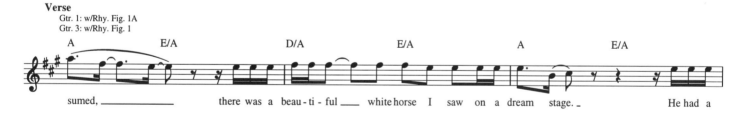

Bridge
Gtr. 3 tacet

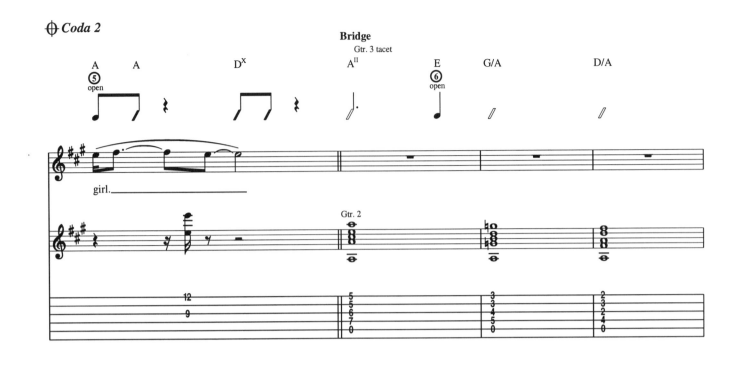

girl._____

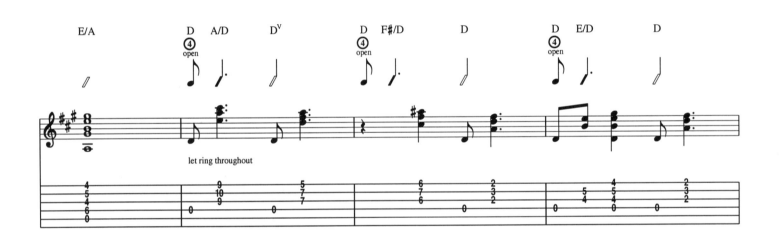

let ring throughout

Look in - to the face of a child, ___ mea - sure how long you smiled

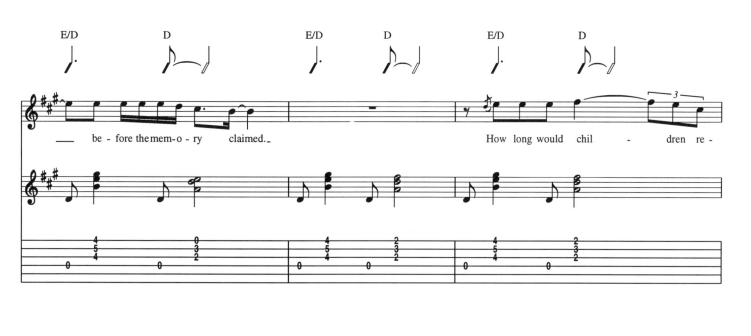

be - fore the mem-o - ry claimed.___ How long would chil - dren re -

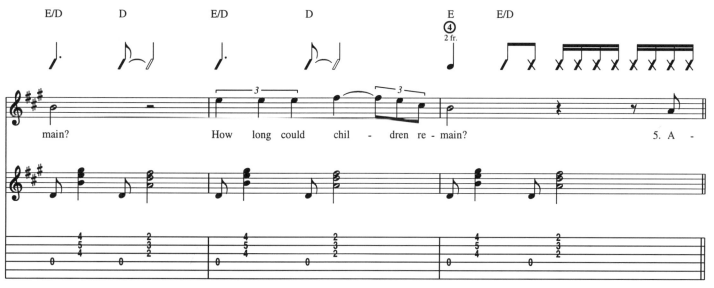

main? How long could chil - dren re - main? 5. A -

Verse

Gtr. 2: tacet
Gtr. 1: w/Rhy. Fig. 1A
Gtr. 3: w/Rhy. Fig. 1

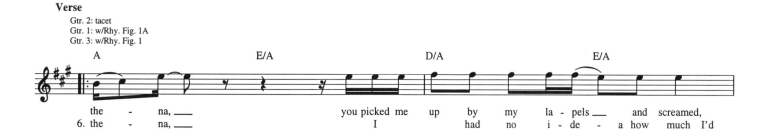

the - na,___ you picked me up by my la - pels___ and screamed,
6. the - na,___ I had no i - de - a how much I'd

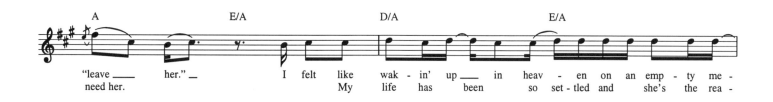

"leave ___ her." ___ I felt like wak - in' up ___ in heav - en on an emp - ty me -
need her. My life has been so set - tled and she's the rea -

___ ter. ___ And now you're stuck with a cas - tra - ted lead - er.___ And I hate the creep.___ She's just a
son. Just one word from her and my trou-bles are long gone. Ooh, but I'll get a-long.___ She's just a

9

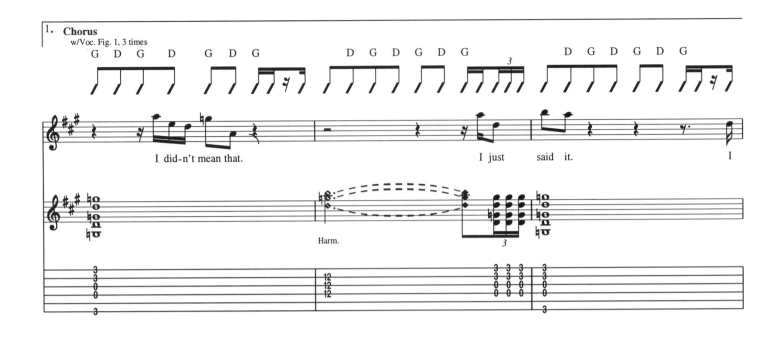

I did-n't mean that.   I just said it.   I

Harm.

did-n't!   Please!   6. A-   girl!

Harm.   Harm.

She's just a   girl!

Baba O'Riley

Words and Music by Peter Townshend

*Violin arr. for gtr.

†Symbols in parenthesis represent chord names respective to capoed guitar
when written in slash notation, and do not reflect actual sounding chords.

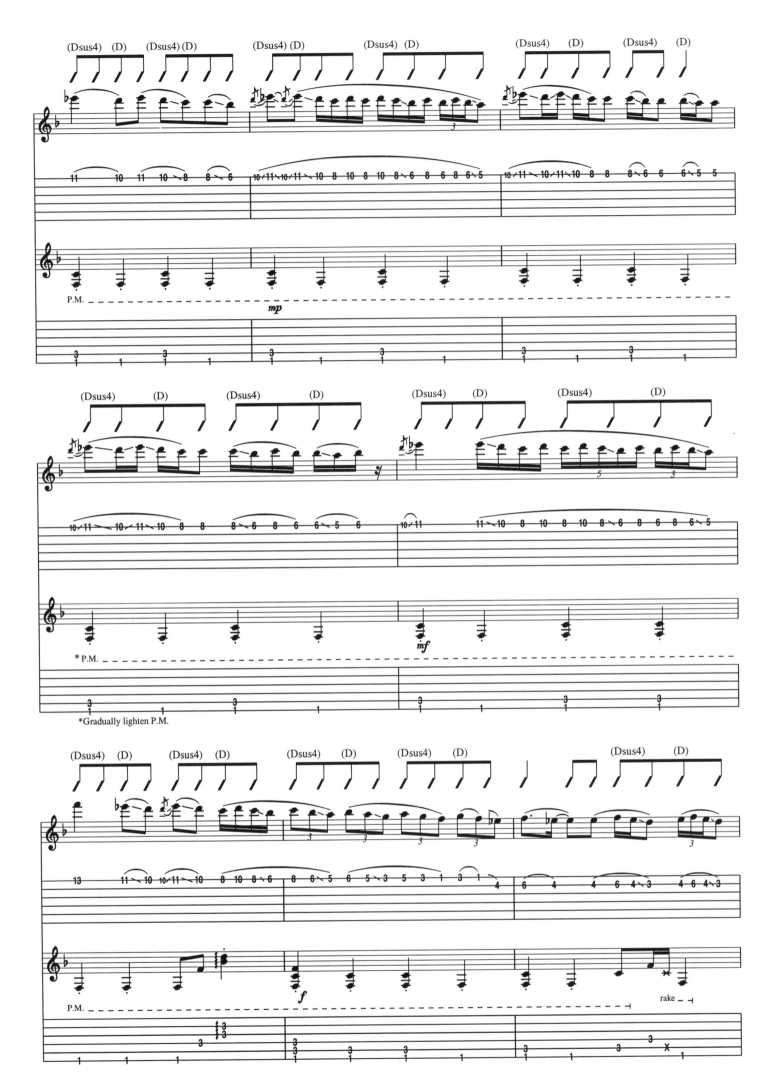

*Release F5 chord when striking ⑥ 1st fret, next 2 meas.

Bargain

Words and Music by Peter Townshend

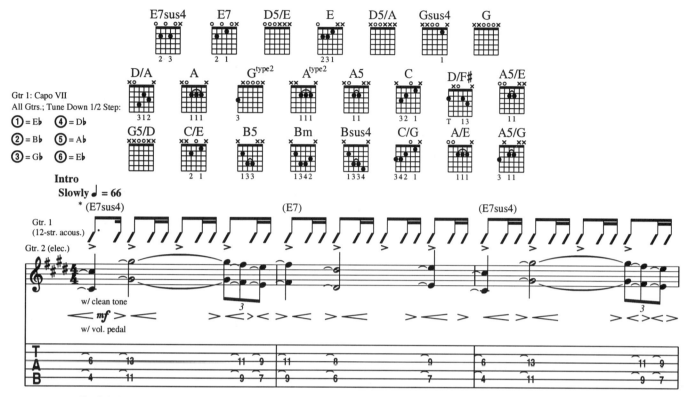

Gtr 1: Capo VII
All Gtrs.; Tune Down 1/2 Step:
① = Eb ④ = Db
② = Bb ⑤ = Ab
③ = Gb ⑥ = Eb

Intro

Slowly ♩ = 66

*(E7sus4)

Gtr. 1
(12-str. acous.)
Gtr. 2 (elec.)

w/ clean tone
mf
w/ vol. pedal

*Symbols in parentheses represent chord names respective to capoed guitar when written in slash notation, and do not reflect actual sounding chords

Verse

Double-Time ♩ = 132

1. I'd glad-ly lose me to find you. I'd glad-ly give up all I have.

P.M.

To find you, I'd suf-fer an-y - thing and be glad. I'll

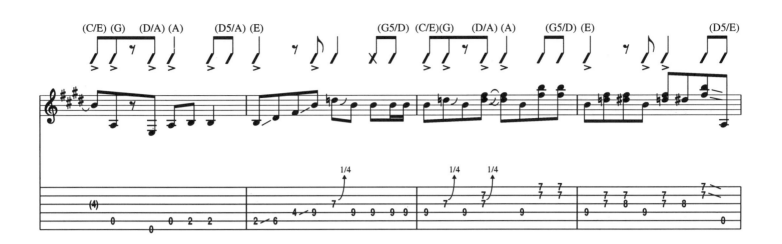

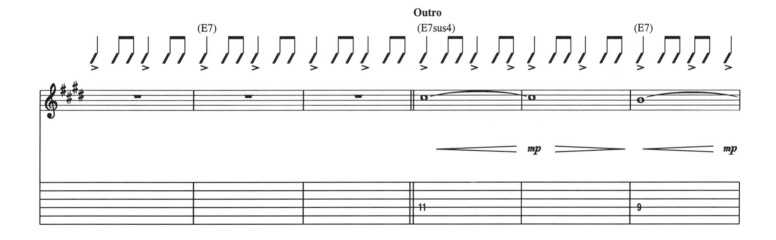

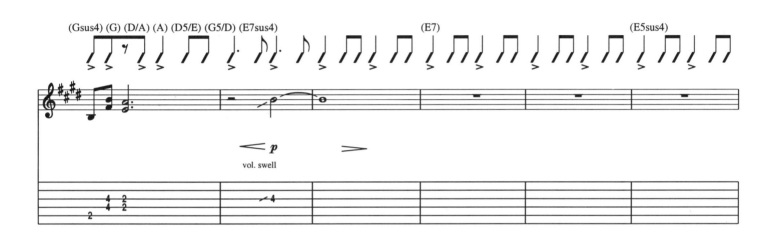

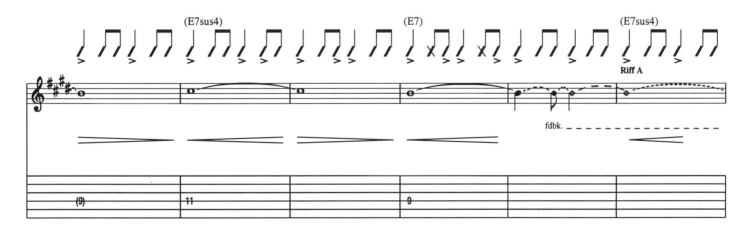

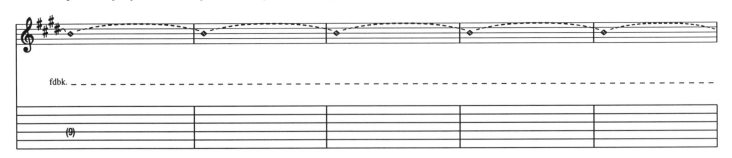

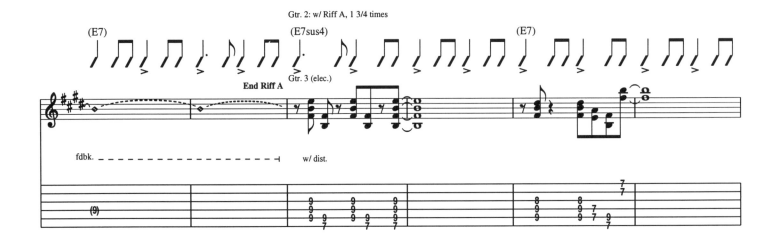

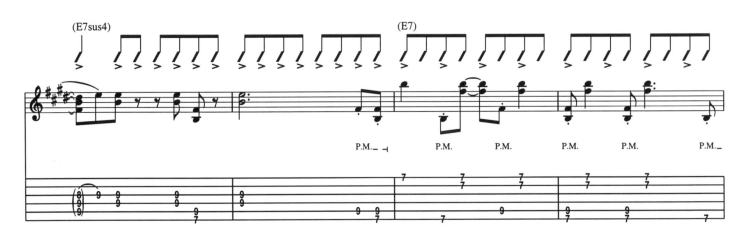

Behind Blue Eyes

Words and Music by Peter Townshend

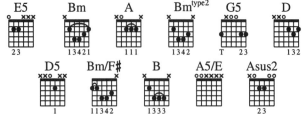

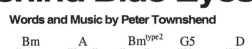

Intro
Moderately Slow ♩ = 60

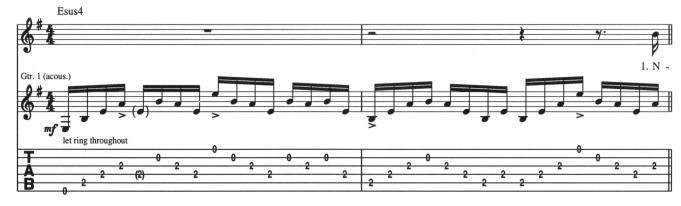

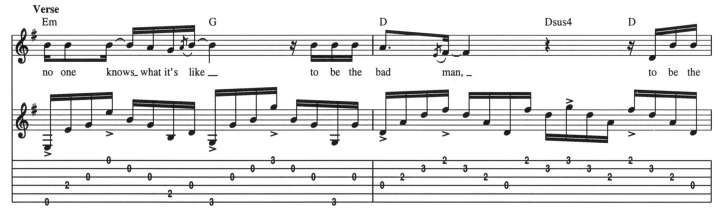

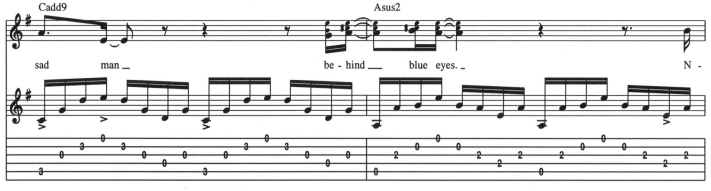

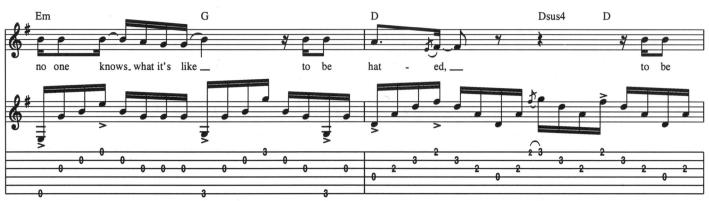

fat - ed ___ to tell - ing on - ly lies. But my

Chorus

dreams, ___ they aren't as emp - ty as my con - science seems ___ to be..

I have hours ___ on - ly lone - ly. ___ My love is ven -

- geance that's nev - er free. 2. N -

-vil, put your fin - ger down my throat. And if I shiv - er, please give me a

Interlude

blan - ket, keep me warm, _ let me wear your coat. _

* vib w/ neck

vib w/ neck

(cont. in notation)

* Vibrato achieved by applying force with right hand on gtr. body & left hand on neck.

Outro
Half-Time ♩ = 60

Gtr. 2 tacet

N - no one knows what it's like __ to be the

Gtr. 1

Gtr. 2

bad man, __ to be the sad man __ be-hind __ blue eyes. __

poco rit.

Gtr. 2

poco rit.

Dogs

Words and Music by Peter Townshend

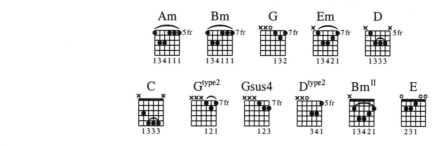

Intro
Moderate ♩ = 126

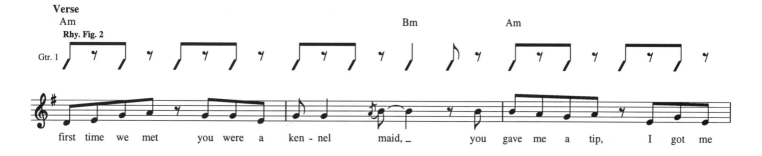

1. The

Verse

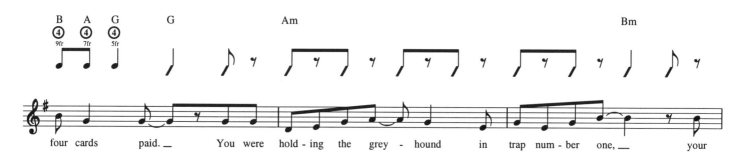

first time we met you were a ken-nel maid,___ you gave me a tip, I got me

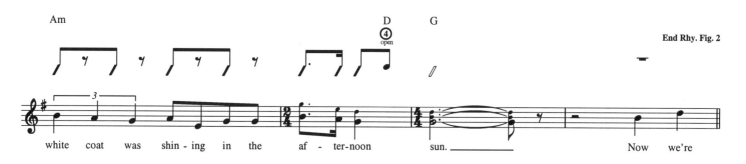

four cards paid.___ You were hold-ing the grey-hound in trap num-ber one,___ your

white coat was shin-ing in the af-ter-noon sun.___ Now we're

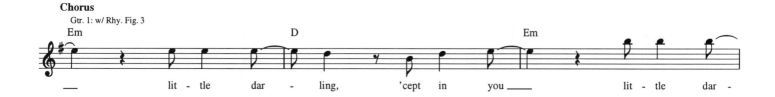

Chorus

Gtr. 1: w/ Rhy. Fig. 3

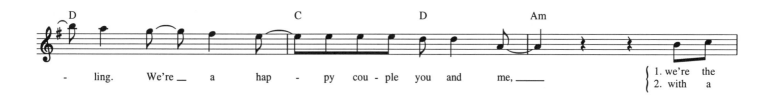

— lit - tle dar - ling, 'cept in you __ lit - tle dar -

- ling. We're __ a hap - py cou - ple you and me, ____

1. we're the
2. with a

grey - hound on ei - ther knee. ____
ba - by on ei - ther knee. ____

1st time only: We

To Coda

Verse

Gtr. 1: w/ Rhy. Fig. 2

go to the dog __ track on Sat - ur - day nights, __ we put all our mon - ey on a

dog that we like. __ A kiss in a car __ door and off we ride, __

take all our tick - ets and a star - ry sky. There was

D.S. al Coda

Coda

Ya da da da __ da ya da da da da da, ya da da da __ da ya da

Gtr. 1

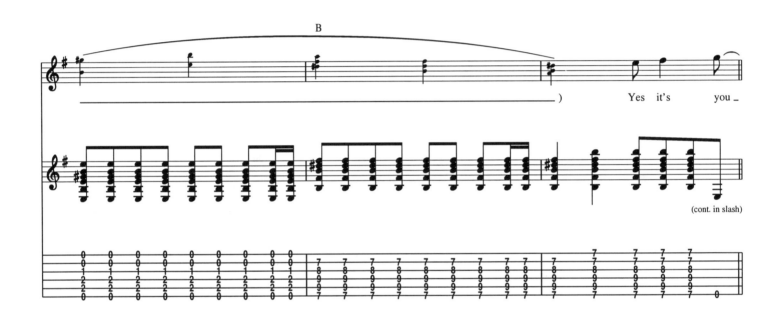

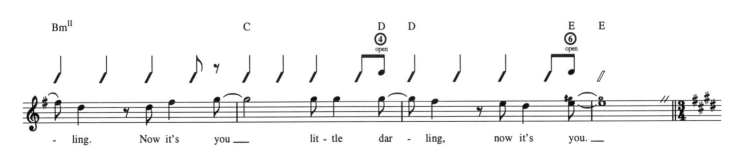

Don't Let Go the Coat

Words and Music by Peter Townshend

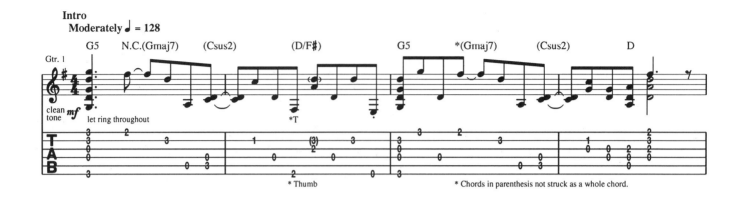

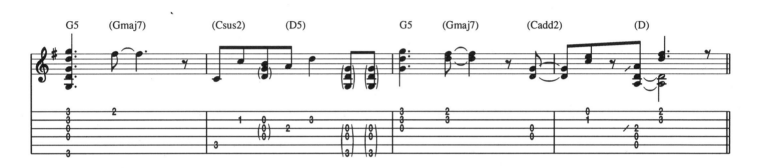

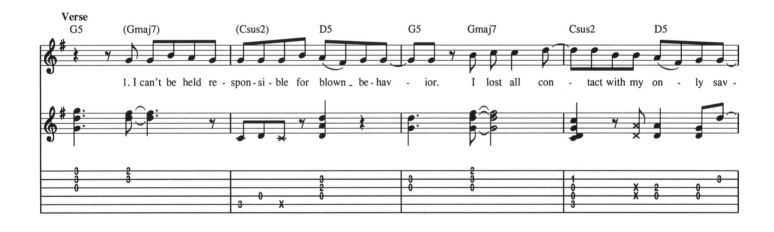

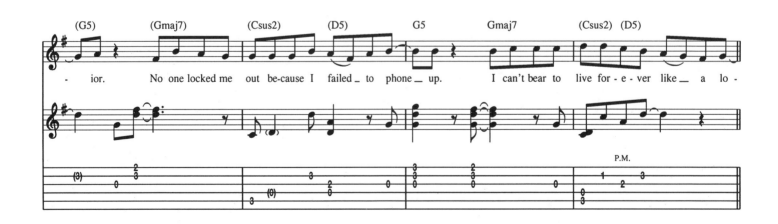

Chorus

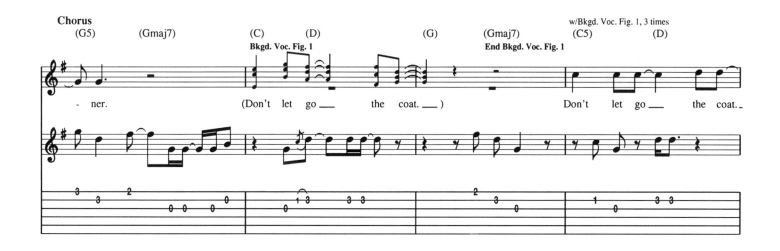

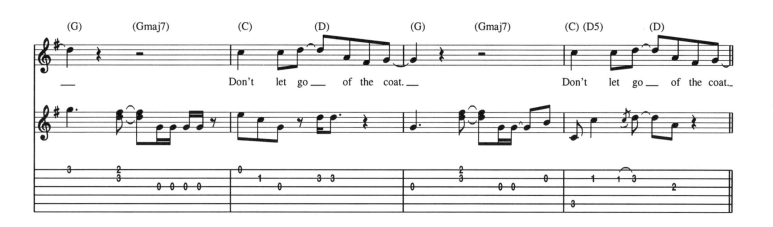

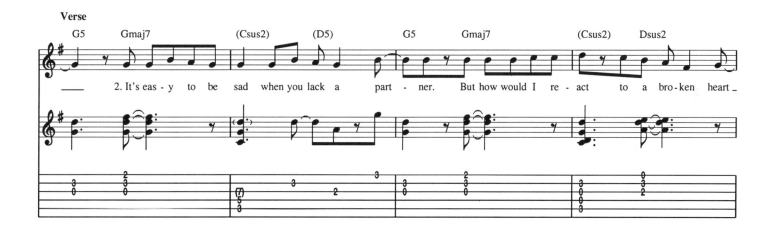

Verse

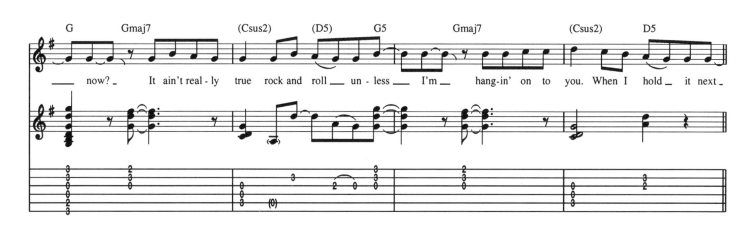

Chorus

— time... I won't let go of the coat.

Don't let go of the coat.

Guitar Solo

* Gtr. 2 (Acous.) indicated to left of slashes in TAB.

* P.M. refers to both gtrs.

Bridge
Half Time ♩ = 64

I try to ex-plain but you nev-er un-der - stand _ it.

I need your bod-y but I can't just de -

(Ooh. _____)

(Ooh. _____

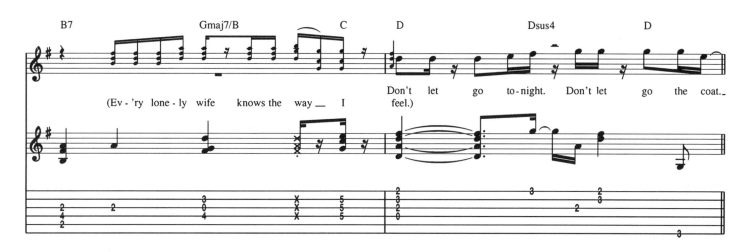

Chorus
Tempo I ♩ = 128

w/Bkgd. Voc. Fig. 1, 4 times

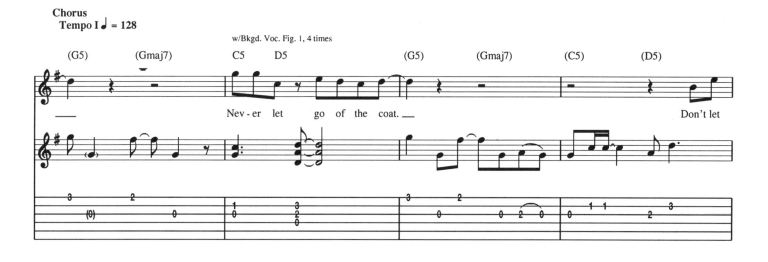

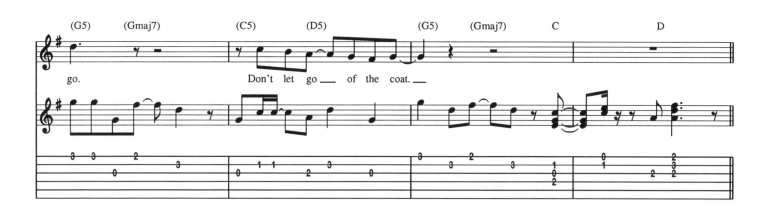

Verse

3. Your friends all pass, ___ for life is just a mar - ket; but you have to fin - ish ev - 'ry - thing ___ you start -

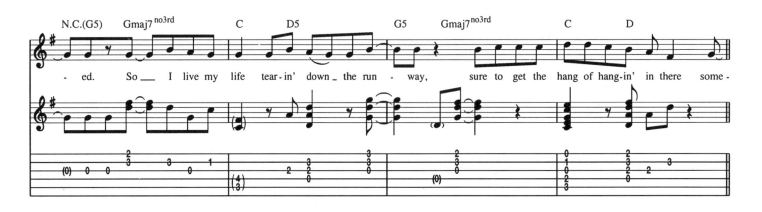

- ed. So ___ I live my life tear - in' down ___ the run - way, sure to get the hang of hang - in' in there some -

Chorus

Gtr. 1: w/Rhy. Fig. 3, 4 times, simile

w/Bkgd. Voc. Fig. 1, till end

day. ___ Don't let go ___ of the coat. ___ Don't let go ___ of the coat. ___

___ Nev - er let go of the coat. ___

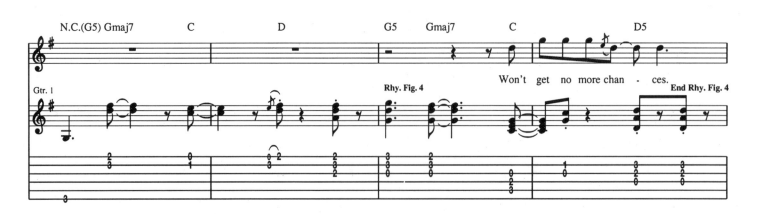

Won't get no more chan - ces.

Gtr. 1: w/ Rhy. Fig. 4, 7 times, simile

Ooh, for - get the war dan - ces. Don't let go. ___ Don't let go. ___

Nev-er let go the coat.   Don't let go.   Go blind and hang _ on. _

Don't try _ the slang, _ son. _____   Nev - er let go of the coat. _

Begin Fade
Gtrs. 2 & 3: w/Rhy. Fill 1   Gtr. 1: w/Rhy. Fig. 3, 2 times, simile

_ No, no.   Don't let go. _   Don't let go of the coat. _

Fade Out

Gtr. 1: w/Rhy. Fig. 4, 1 1/2 times

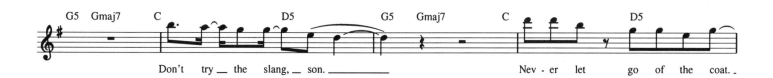

_ Don't let go.   Don't let go of the coat. __   Nev - er let go. ___

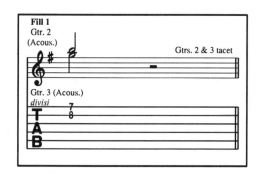

Fill 1
Gtr. 2
(Acous.)
Gtrs. 2 & 3 tacet
Gtr. 3 (Acous.)
divisi

Rhy. Fill 1
Gtrs. 2 & 3
let ring throughout

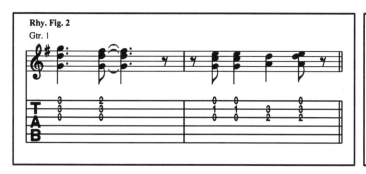

Rhy. Fig. 2
Gtr. 1

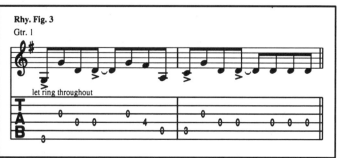

Rhy. Fig. 3
Gtr. 1
let ring throughout

Eminence Front

Words and Music by Peter Townshend

50

Fill 1
Gtr. 1

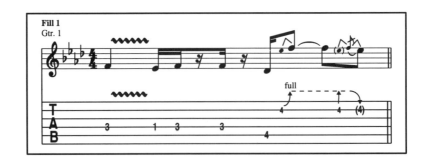

Fill 2
Gtr. 1

Fill 3
Gtr. 1

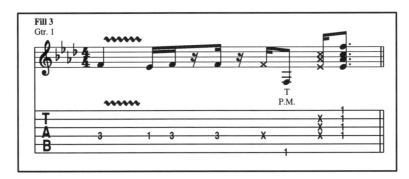

Fill 4
Gtr. 1

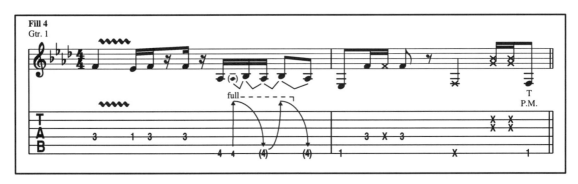

Fill 5
Gtr. 1

Fill 6
Gtr. 1

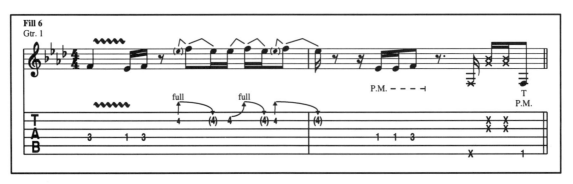

5:15

Words and Music by Peter Townshend

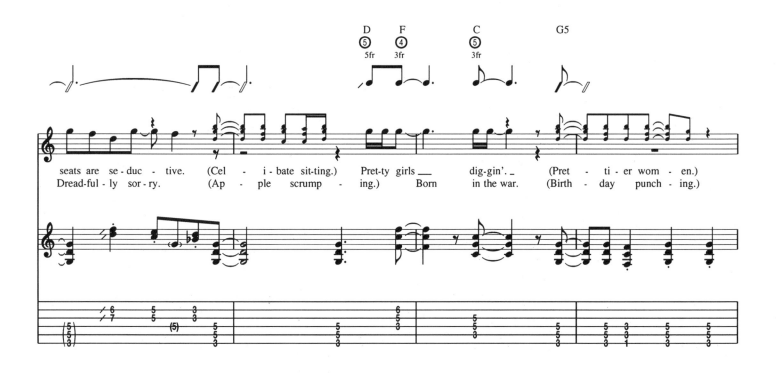

seats are se-duc-tive. (Cel - i-bate sit-ting.) Pret-ty girls ___ dig-gin'. ___ (Pret - ti-er wom - en.)
Dread-ful-ly sor-ry. (Ap - ple scrump - ing.) Born in the war. (Birth - day punch - ing.)

Gtr. 1: w/ Rhy. Fig. 3, 7 times
Gtr. 2: w/ Rhy. Fig. 5, 2nd time, 3 times
Gtr. 2: w/ Fill 3, 2nd time

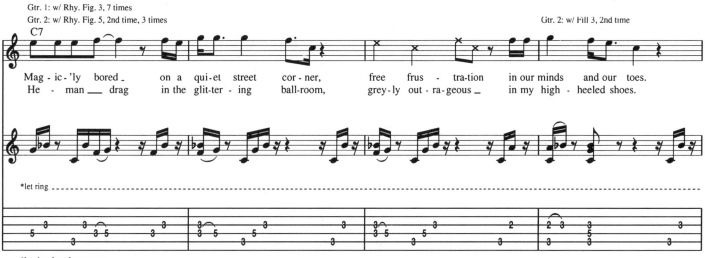

Mag - ic-'ly bored ___ on a qui-et street cor - ner, free frus - tra-tion in our minds and our toes.
He - man ___ drag in the glit-ter - ing ball-room, grey-ly out - ra-geous ___ in my high - heeled shoes.

*let ring -

*let ring, but observe rests

Gtr. 2: w/ Rhy. Fig. 5, 2nd time
Gtr. 2: w/ Fill 5, 2nd time
Gtr. 2: w/ Fill 4, 2nd time
Gtr. 2: w/ Rhy. Fig. 5, 2nd time

Qui - et storm - wa - ter, m-m-my gen - er - a - tion. Up - pers and down-ers; eith - er way, blood flows. ___
Tight-ly un - done, they know what they're show - ing. Sad - ly ec - stat - ic that their he - roes _____ are _

*let ring -

Interlude

Gtr. 3: w/ Rhy. Fig. 2, 4 times
Gtr. 4: w/ Riff A, 4 times

Chorus

Gtrs. 1 & 3 tacet

In - side, out - side, __ leave me a - lone.. In - side, out - side, __ no-where is home..

In - side, out - side, __ where have I been? __ Out of my brain __ on the five __ fif - teen..

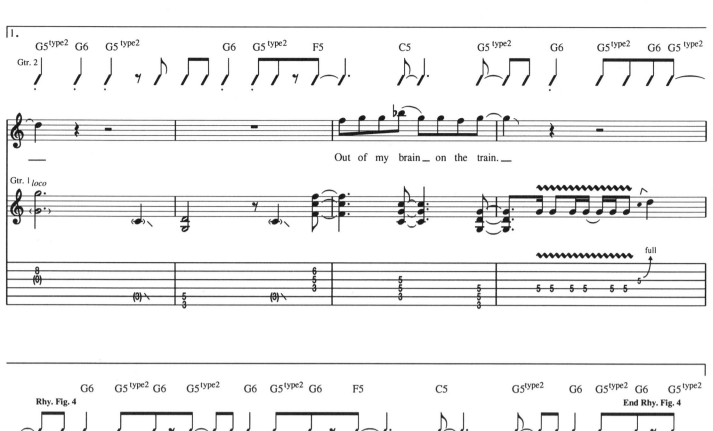

Out of my brain___ on the train.___

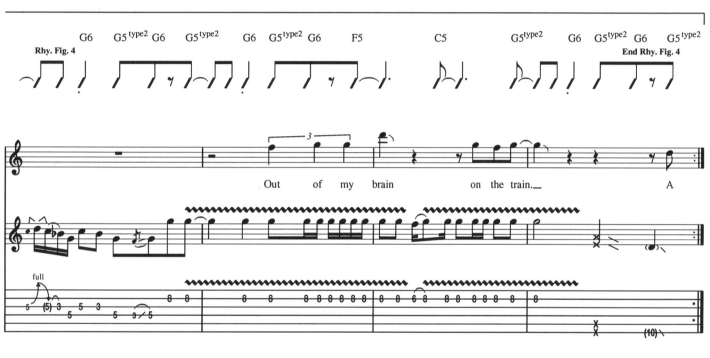

Out of my brain on the train.___ A

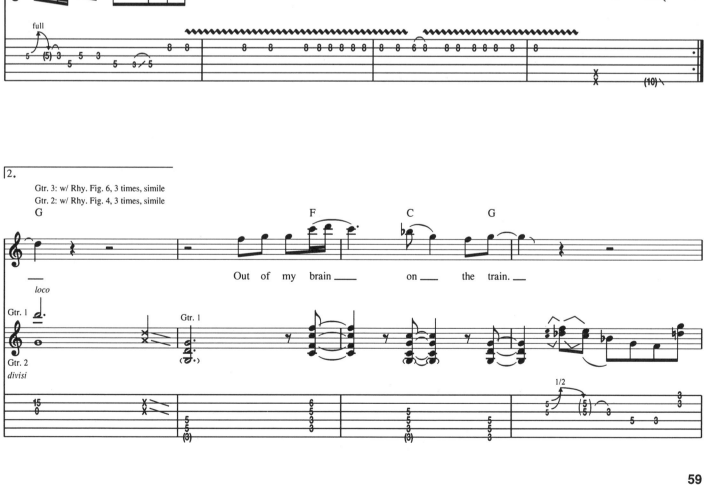

Gtr. 3: w/ Rhy. Fig. 6, 3 times, simile
Gtr. 2: w/ Rhy. Fig. 4, 3 times, simile

Out of my brain_____ on _____ the train.___

Out of my brain _ on the train, _ on the train. Wow. _ I'm out _ of my brain. Woo!

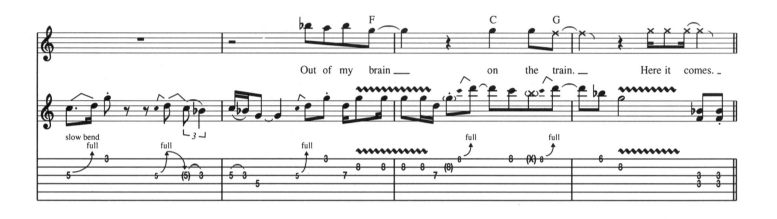

Out of my brain _____ on the train. _ Here it comes. _

Guitar Solo

Gtr. 2: w/ Rhy. Fig. 4, 6 times simile

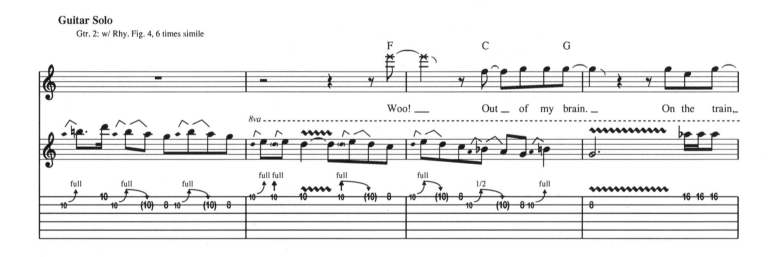

Woo! _ Out _ of my brain. _ On the train, _

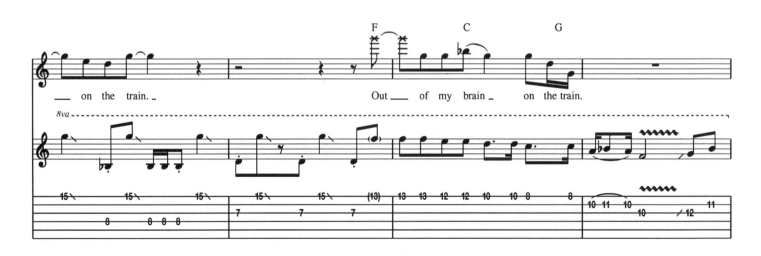

_ on the train. _ Out _ of my brain _ on the train.

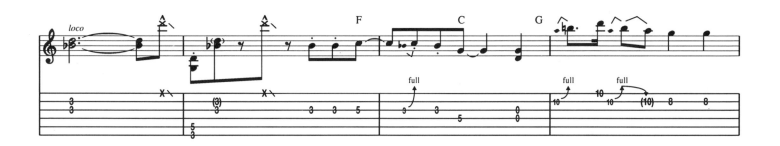

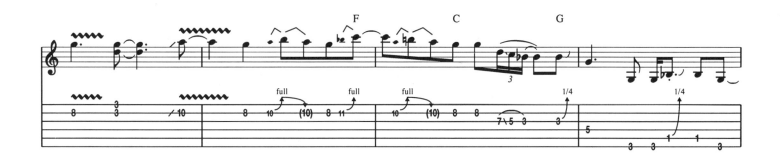

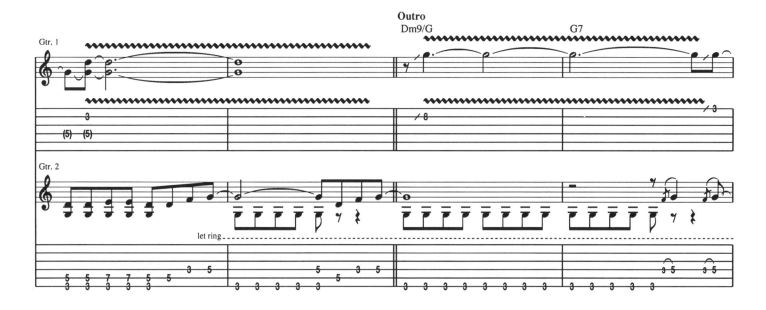

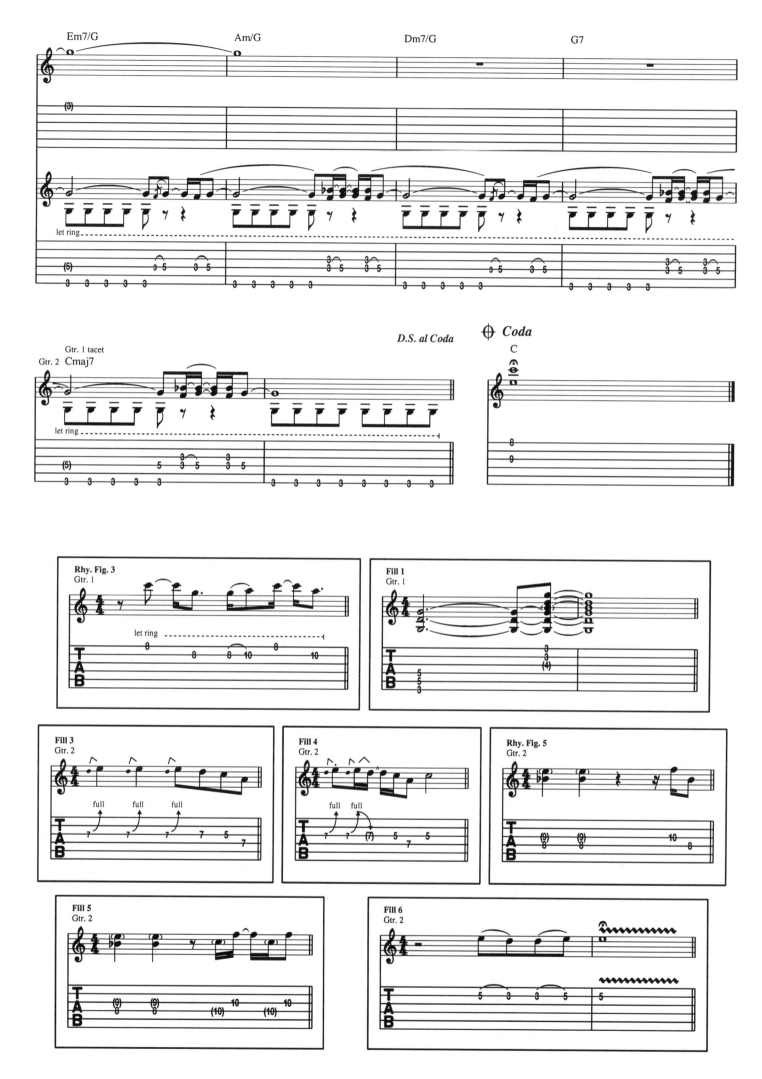

Going Mobile

Words and Music by Peter Townshend

*Symbols in parentheses represent chord names respective to capoed gtr. Symbols above reflect actual sounding chord.

*Pick mute str. while moving L.H. toward 12th fret.

*Release finger pressure to mute str. and pick while sliding down.

Additional Lyrics

3. Play the tape machine, make the toast and tea when I'm mobile.
   Well, I can lay in bed with only highway ahead when I'm mobile.
   Keep me movin'.

I Can See for Miles

Words and Music by Peter Townshend

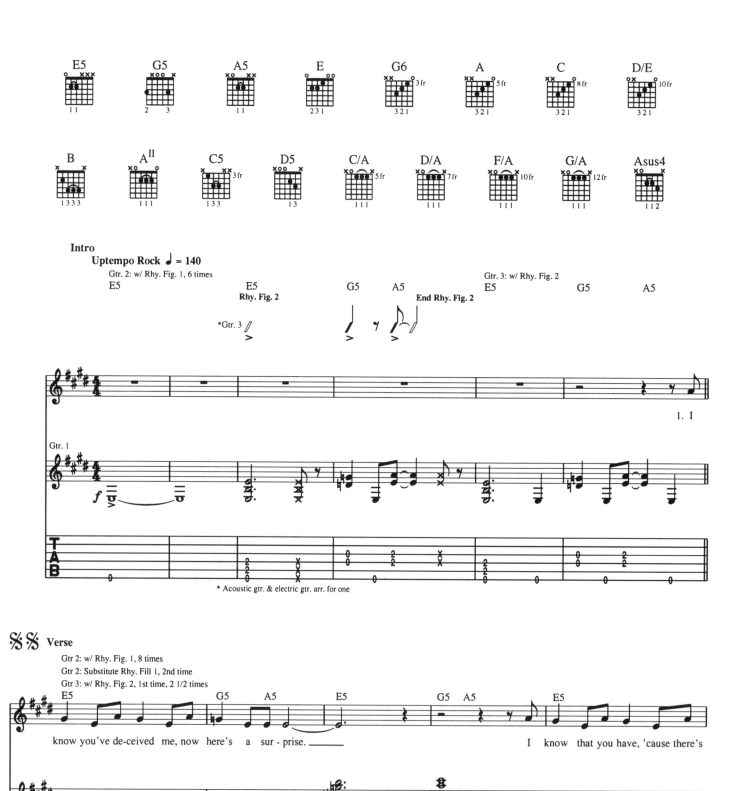

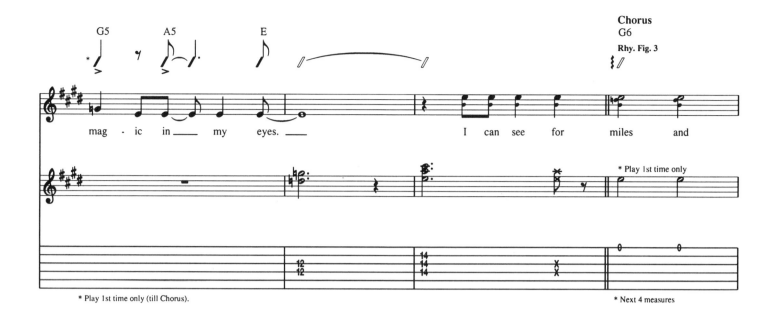

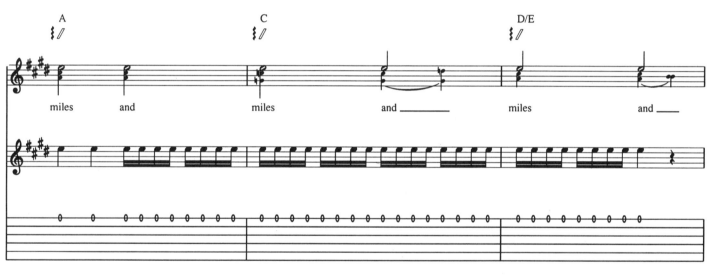

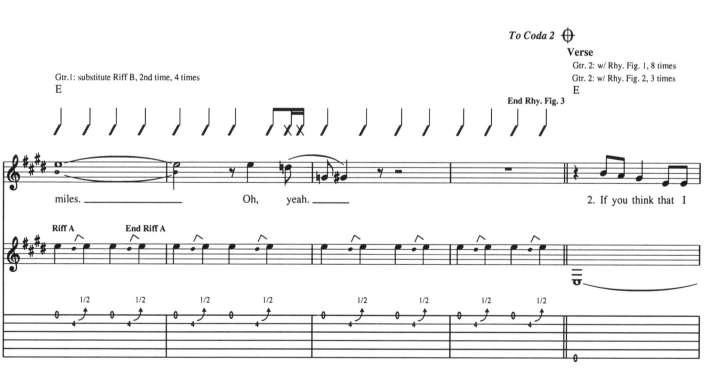

don't know a-bout the lit-tle tricks _ you play _   and nev-er see you when de - lib·'rate-ly you put things in _

Pre-Chorus

_ my way. _   Well, here's a poke at you. _ You're gon-na choke on it, too. _ You're gon-na

𝄋 Chorus

Gtr. 1: w/ Riff A, 1st time, 12 times
Gtr. 1: w/ Riff B, 2nd time, 9 times

lose that smile, _   be - cause all the while,   I can see for miles   and

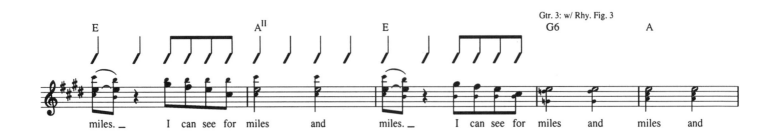

Gtr. 3: w/ Rhy. Fig. 3

miles. _   I can see for miles   and   miles. _   I can see for miles   and   miles   and

To Coda 1 ⊕

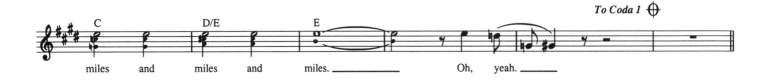

miles   and   miles   and   miles. _____   Oh, yeah. _____

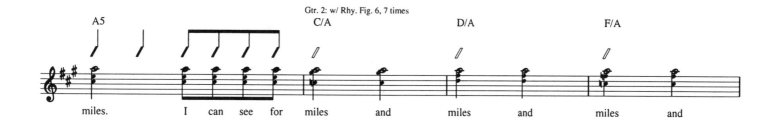

Gtr. 2: w/ Rhy. Fig. 6, 7 times

A5 · · C/A · D/A · F/A

miles. I can see for miles and miles and miles and

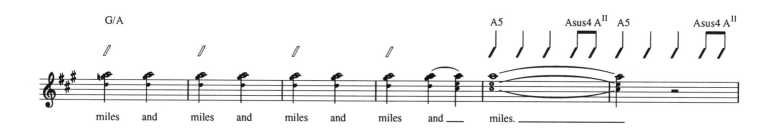

G/A A5 Asus4 A^II A5 Asus4 A^II

miles and miles and miles and miles and ___ miles. ___

Repeat and Fade

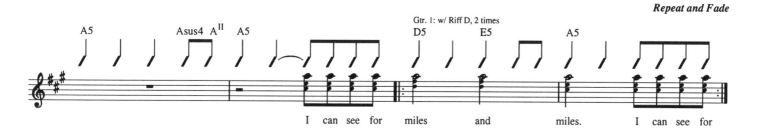

A5 Asus4 A^II A5 Gtr. 1: w/ Riff D, 2 times
D5 E5 A5

I can see for miles and miles. I can see for

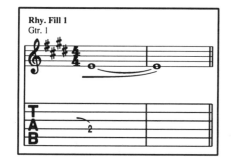

Rhy. Fill 1
Gtr. 1

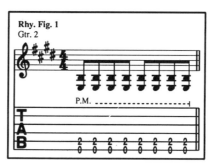

Rhy. Fig. 1
Gtr. 2

P.M. ----------------

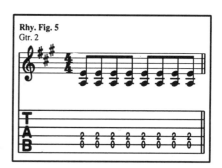

Rhy. Fig. 5
Gtr. 2

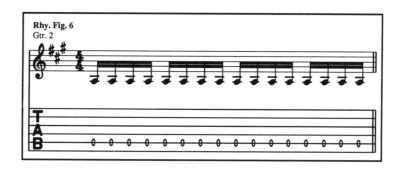

Rhy. Fig. 6
Gtr. 2

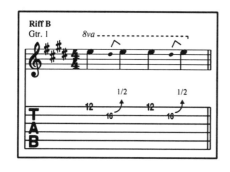

Riff B
Gtr. 1
8va ----------------
1/2   1/2
12 10 12 10

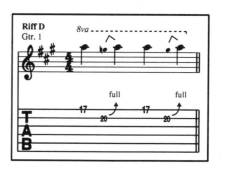

Riff D
Gtr. 1
8va ----------------
full   full
17 20 17 20

I Can't Reach You

Words and Music by Peter Townshend

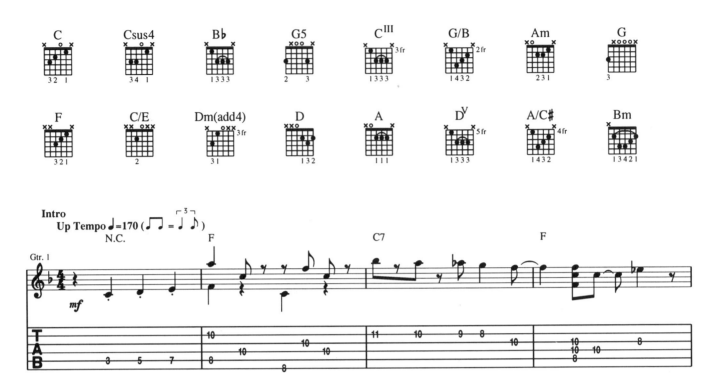

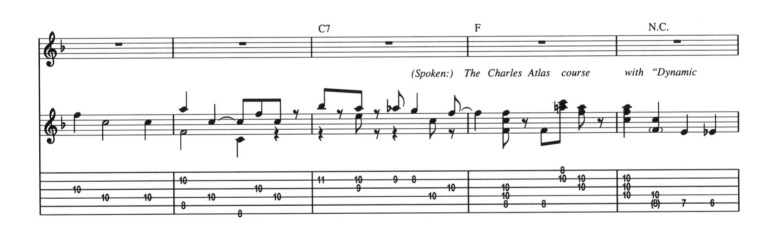

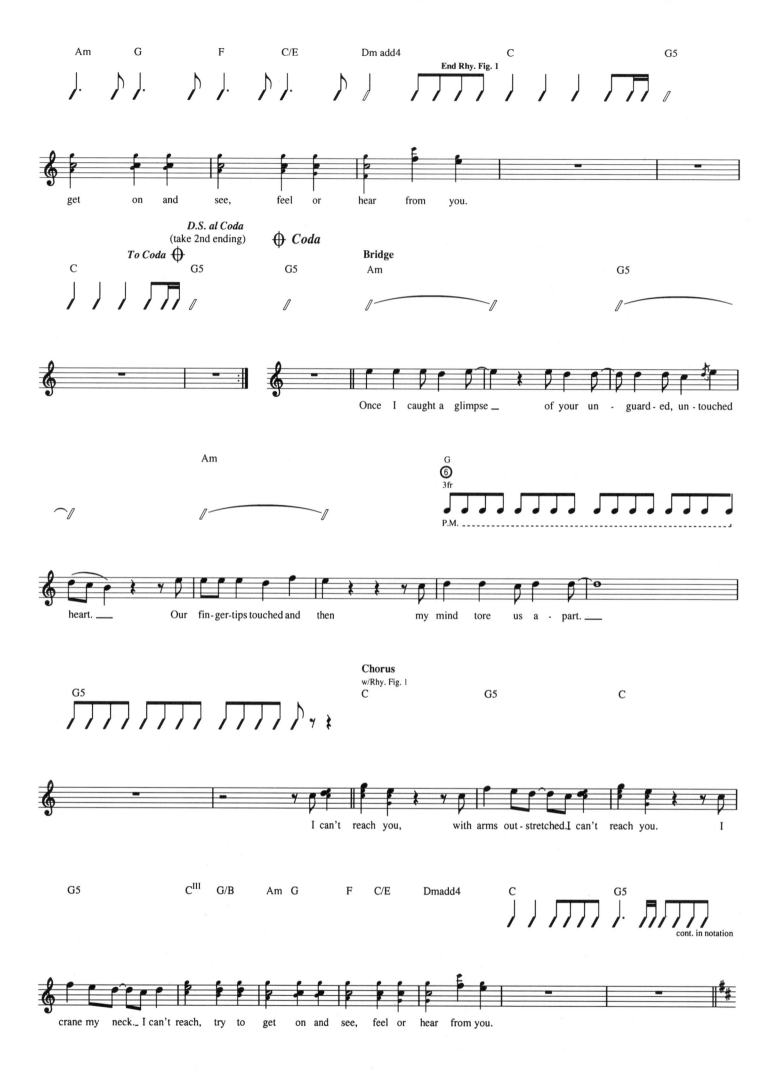

get on and see, feel or hear from you.

To Coda

Coda

Bridge

Once I caught a glimpse _ of your un- guard-ed, un-touched

heart. ___ Our fin-ger-tips touched and then my mind tore us a - part. ___

Chorus
w/Rhy. Fig. 1

I can't reach you, with arms out-stretched. I can't reach you. I

crane my neck.. I can't reach, try to get on and see, feel or hear from you.

I'm Free

Words and Music by Peter Townshend

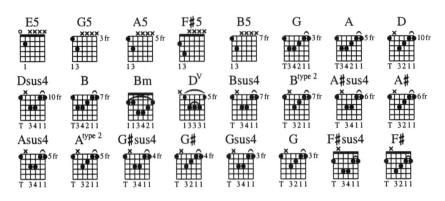

I'm free. __ I'm __ free, __ and free-dom tastes __ of re - al - i - ty. __ I'm __ free. __ I'm __ free, __ and I'm wait - ing __ for you __ to fol - low me. If I told you what it takes. to reach the high-est high, __ you'd laugh and say noth-in's that sim-ple. (Ah. _____) But you've been told man-y times be-fore, mes - si - ah's point-ed to the door. __

No one had the guts_ to leave the tem - ple.
(Ah. _____)
I'm _ free. _ I'm _

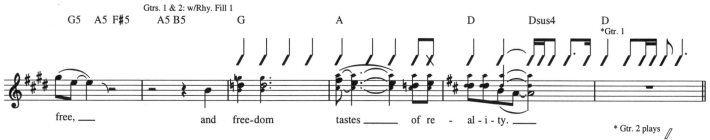

Gtrs. 1 & 2: w/Rhy. Fill 1

free, ___ and free-dom tastes ___ of re - al - i - ty. ___

* Gtr. 2 plays

Guitar Solo

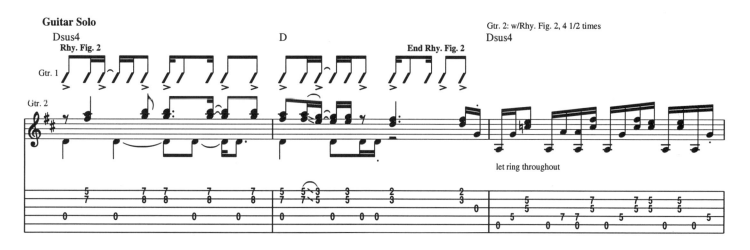

let ring throughout

*Don't let ring.

The Kids Are Alright

Words and Music by Peter Townshend

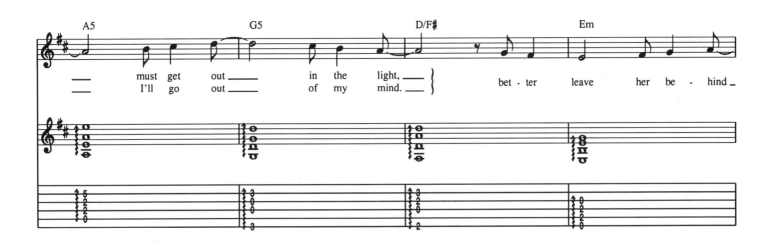

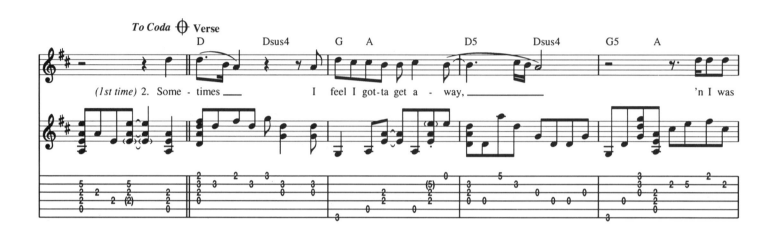

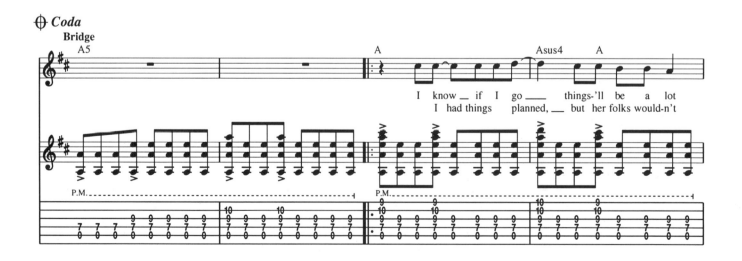

Long Live Rock

Words and Music by Peter Townshend

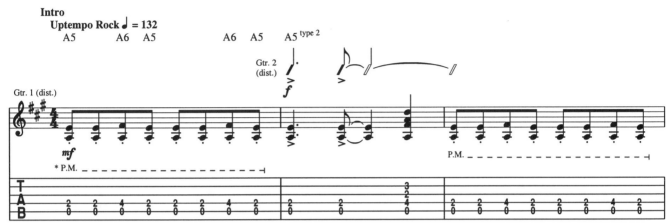

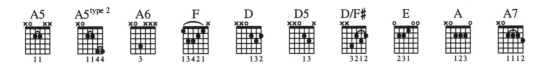

The Magic Bus

Words and Music by Peter Townshend

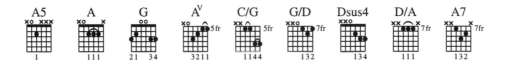

(Tune Down 3/4 Step)

1. Ev-'ry day _ I get in the queue _ (Too much, the mag-ic bus.) to

My Generation

Words and Music by Peter Townshend

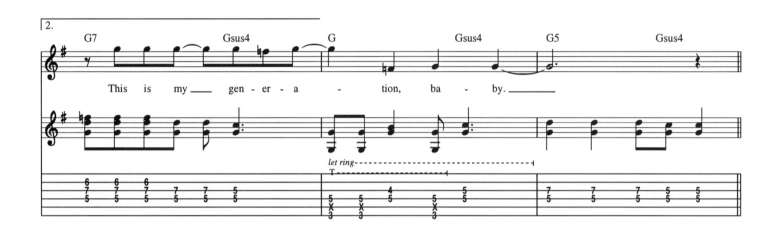

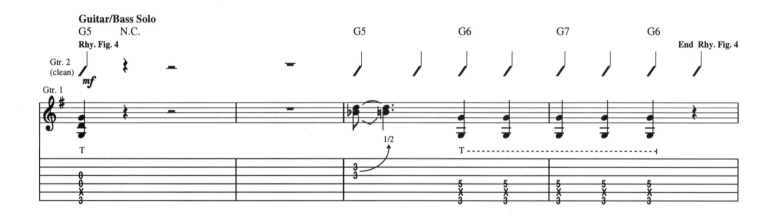

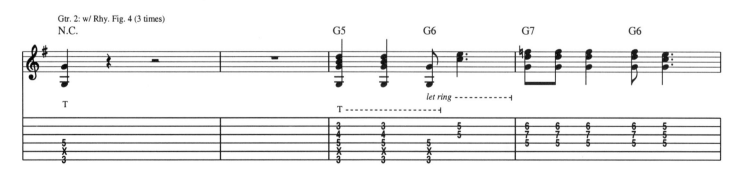

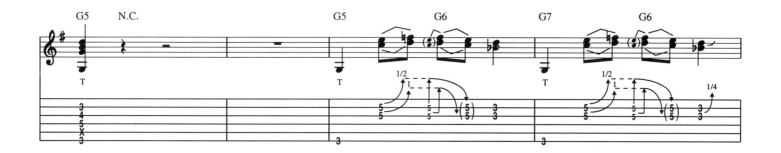

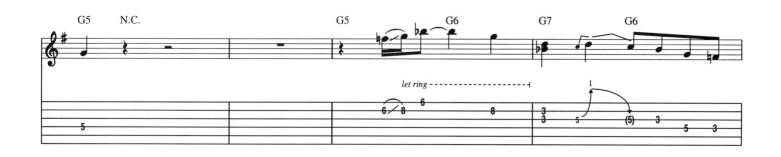

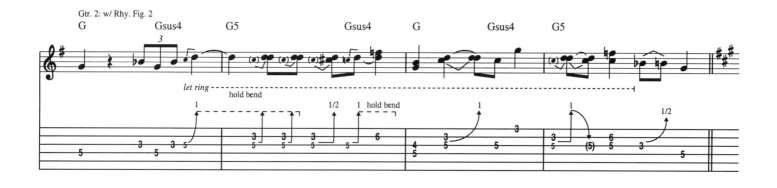

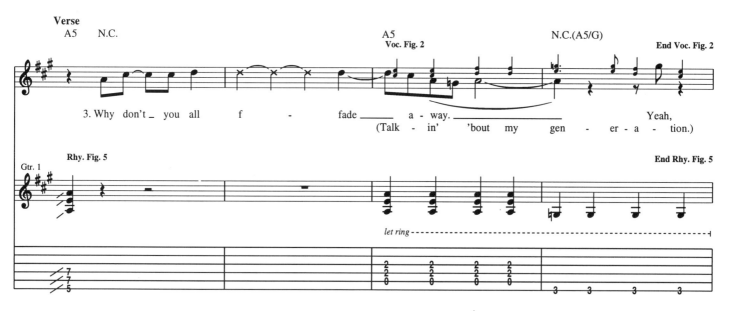

Verse

3. Why don't you all f - fade a - way. Yeah,
(Talk - in' 'bout my gen - er - a - tion.)

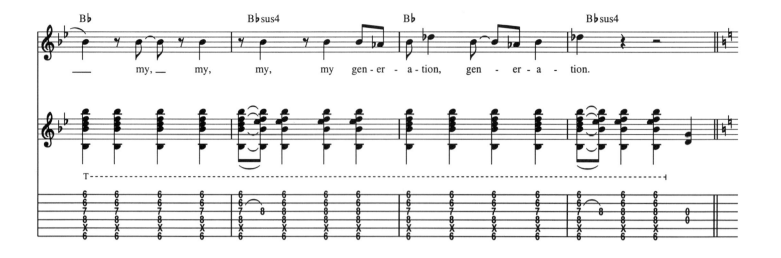

my, — my, my, my gen-er - a-tion, gen - er - a - tion.

Guitar Solo

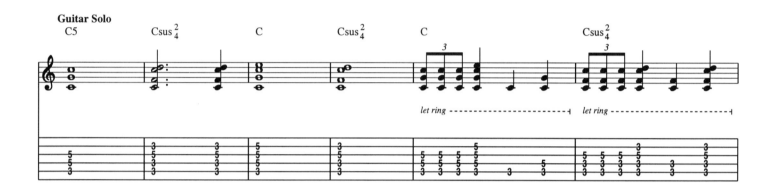

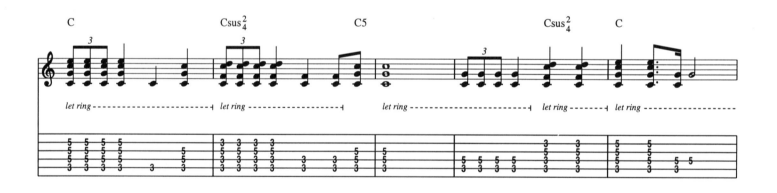

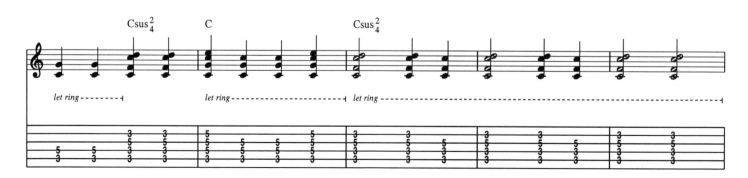

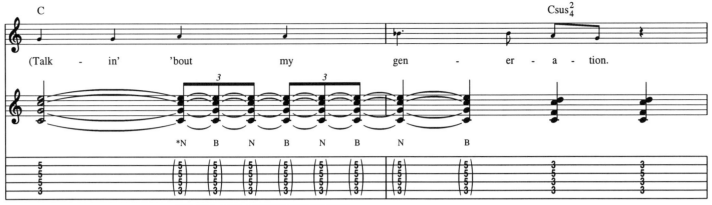

*Flip pickup selector switch from the neck pickup to
 bridge pickup in the specified rhythm to simulate the reattack.

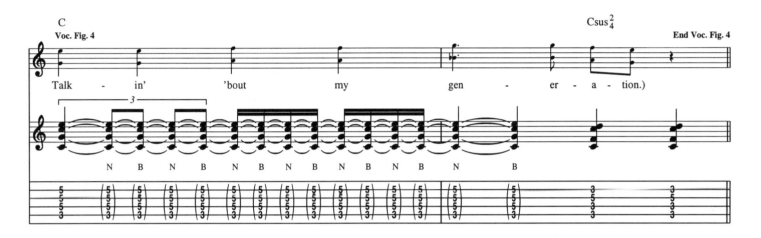

Outro

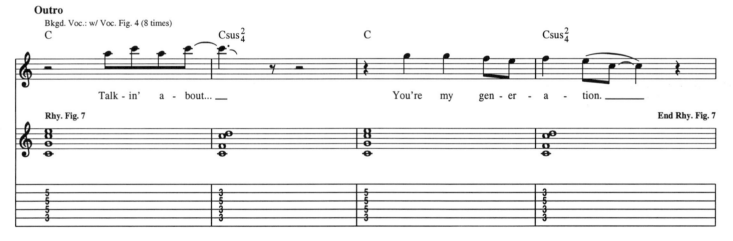

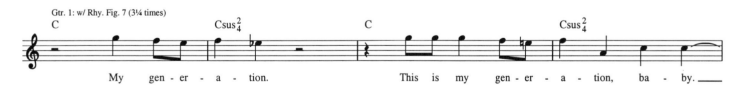

My Wife

Words and Music by John Entwistle

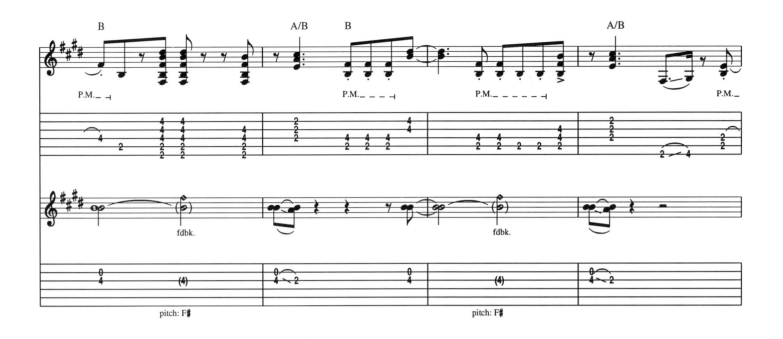

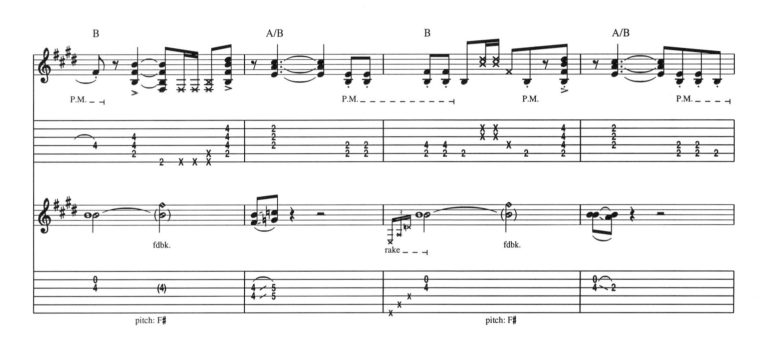

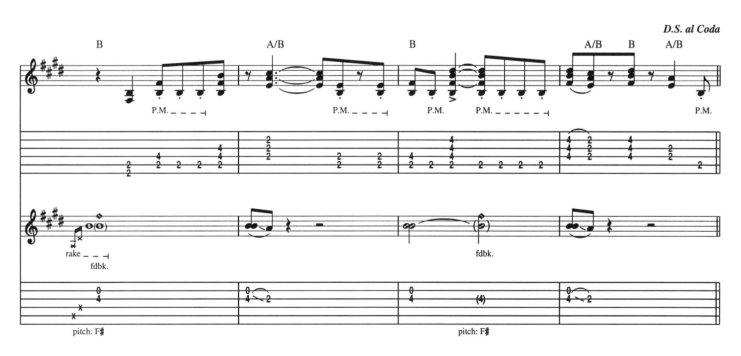

Pinball Wizard

Words and Music by Peter Townshend

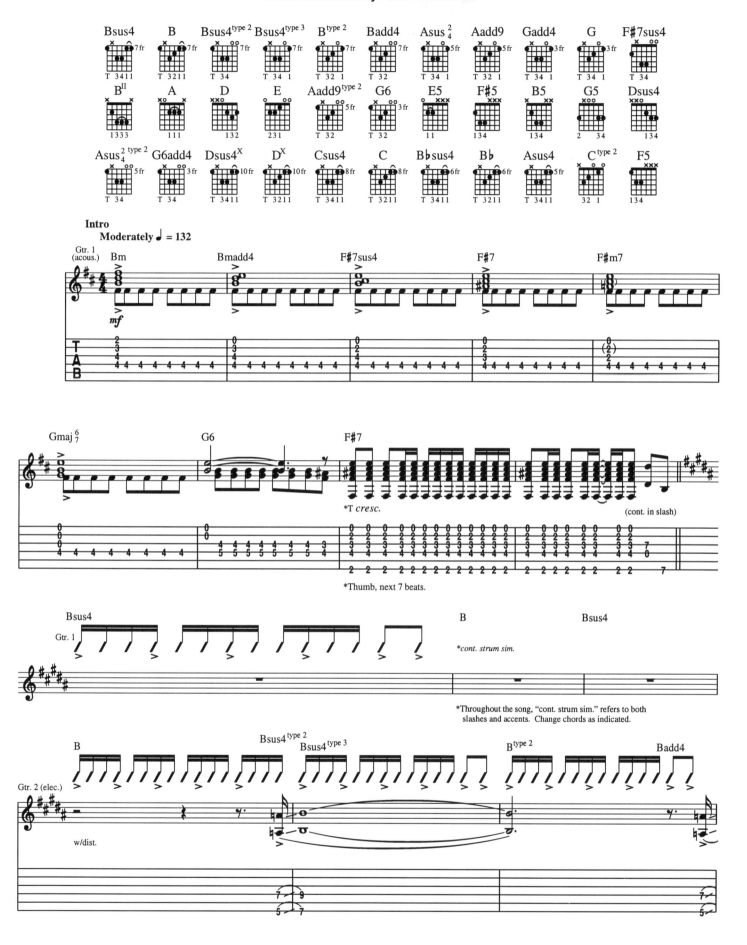

4. E-ven on my fav-rite ta-ble, he can beat my best. His di-sci-ples lead him in_ and he just does the rest.__ He's got cra-zy flip-per fin-gers, nev-er seen him fall._ That deaf, dumb and blind_ kid sure plays a mean pin-ball.

* let ring throughout

*Lower Gtr.'s vol. knob to reduce distortion level.

Begin Fade

cont. strum sim.

Fade Out

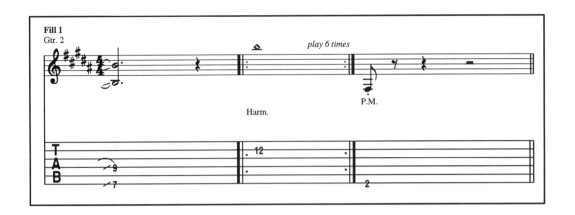

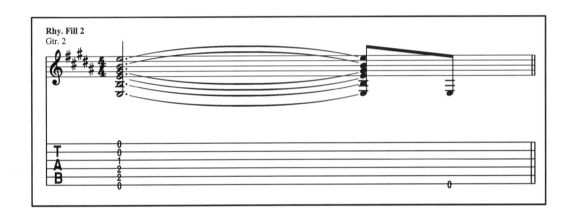

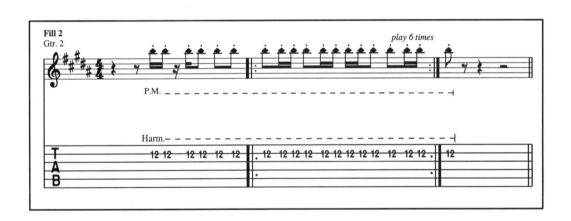

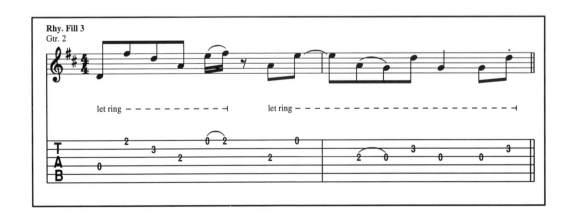

The Real Me

Words and Music by Peter Townshend

Can you see the real ___ me, ___ can ___ ya, can ___ ya?

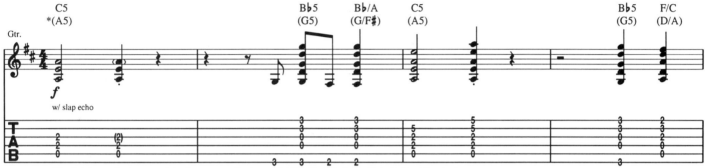

*Symbols in parentheses represent chord names respective to capoed guitar. Symbols above reflect actual sounding chord.

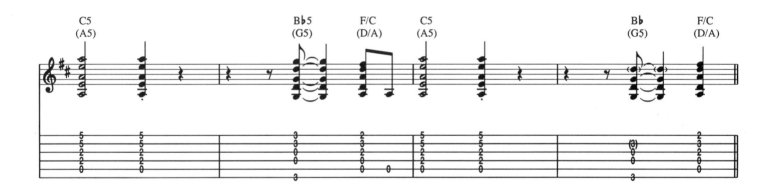

1. I went back ___ to the doc - tor   to get an-oth - er shrink. ___   I sit and
2. I went back ___ to my moth - er,   I said, "I'm cra - zy Ma, help me."   She said,
(4.) girl   I   used to love   lives   in   this yel - low house. ___

Can you see the real _____ me, _ doc - tor?

Can you see the real _

let ring throughout

Free Time

F5/C
(D5/A)

N.C.

echoes keep repeating and fade into "Quadrophenia"

_____ me moth - er? Can you see _ the real me? Me, me, me, me, me, me, *etc.*

Echo repeats -

* -

* Echo repeats from final chord hit. Extend approximately 6 beats, and then fade.

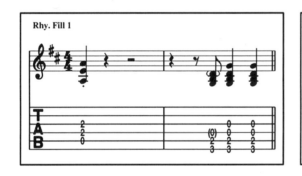

Rhy. Fill 1

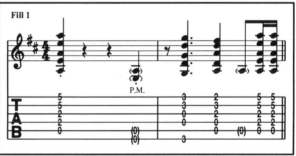

Fill 1

P.M.

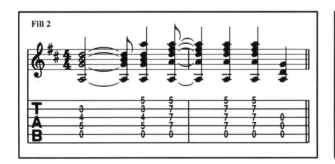

Fill 2

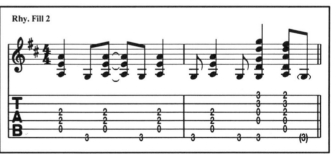

Rhy. Fill 2

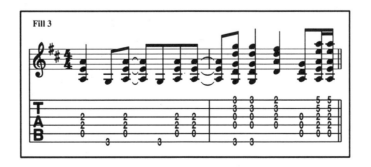

Fill 3

The Seeker

Words and Music by Peter Townshend

I won't get to get what I'm af-ter 'til the day I die.

Coda 1

Verse

why. 3. I'm look-in' for me,__ you're look-in' for you.__ We're look-in' in at each oth-er and we

Coda 2

don't know what to do.__ They call me the

Rhy. Fill 1

Rhy. Fill 2

Rhy. Fill 3

Rhy. Fill 4

Squeeze Box

Words and Music by Peter Townshend

Substitute

Words and Music by Peter Townshend

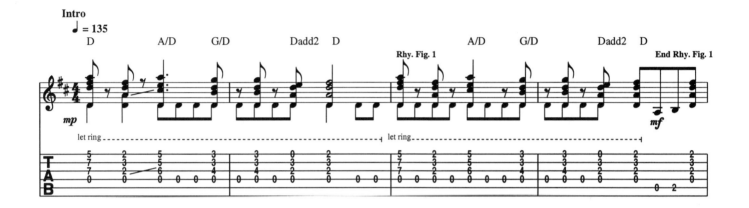

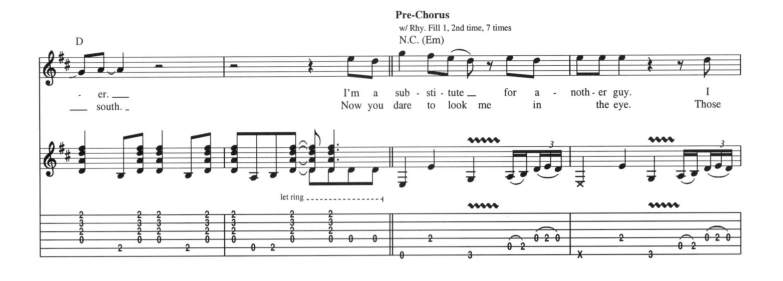

Pre-Chorus
w/ Rhy. Fill 1, 2nd time, 7 times

N.C. (Em)

I'm a sub-sti-tute ___ for a-noth-er guy. I
Now you dare to look me in the eye. Those

look pret-ty tall but my heels are high. The sim-ple things ya' see are all com-pli-ca-ted. (I
croc-o-dile tears are what you cry. It's a gen-u-ine prob-lem. You won't try ___ to

look blood-y young but I'm just back-dat-ed, yeah.
work it out at all; you just pass it by, pass it by. ___

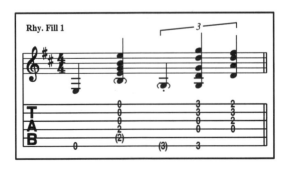

Rhy. Fill 1

Chorus

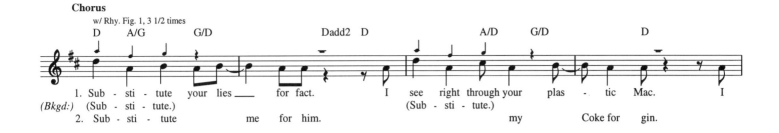

1. Sub - sti - tute your lies ___ for fact. I see right through your plas - tic Mac. I
(Bkgd:) (Sub - sti - tute.) (Sub - sti - tute.)
2. Sub - sti - tute me for him. my Coke for gin.

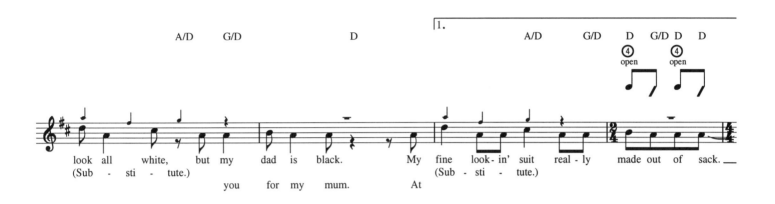

look all white, but my dad is black. My fine look-in' suit real - ly made out of sack. ___
(Sub - sti - tute.) (Sub - sti - tute.)
you for my mum. At

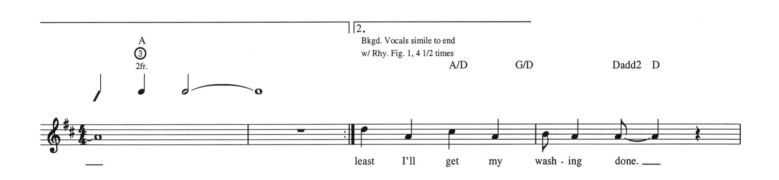

least I'll get my wash - ing done. ___

Bkgd. Vocals simile to end
w/ Rhy. Fig. 1, 4 1/2 times

mp Sub - sti - tute your lies ___ for fact. I see right through your plas - tic Mac. I

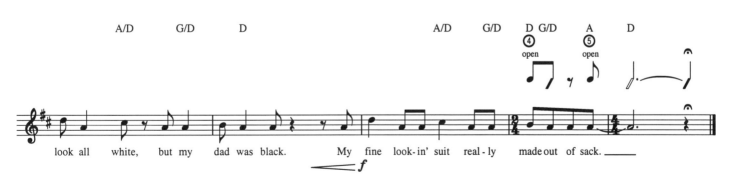

look all white, but my dad was black. My fine look-in' suit real - ly made out of sack. ___

Who Are You

Words and Music by Peter Townshend

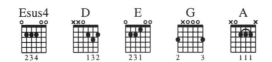

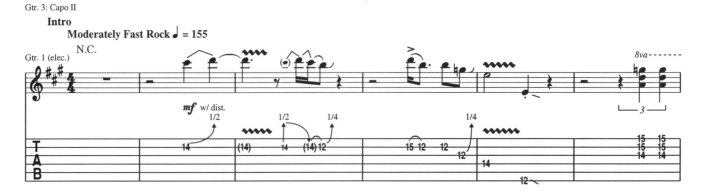

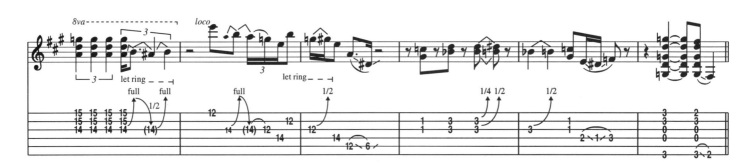

Verse
Half-Time Feel
Gtr. 2 tacet

1. I woke up in a So-ho door-way, a po-lice-man knew my name. He said, "You can go sleep at home
2., 3. *See Additional Lyrics*

Gtr. 1

simile 2nd & 3rd times

— to-night — if you can get up and walk — a-way." — I stag-gered back to the un-der-ground — and the breeze —

'cause I real-ly want to know.

2.

Chorus
w/ Voc. Fig. 1, 4 times
Gtr. 2: w/ Rhy. Fig. 1, simile

you?

Oh, _____ who are

you?

C' - mon, tell me who are

you.

Oh, who the fuck are

*Chord symbol reflects combined tonality.

** knock on gtr.'s body

* knock on gtr.'s body

Half-Time Feel

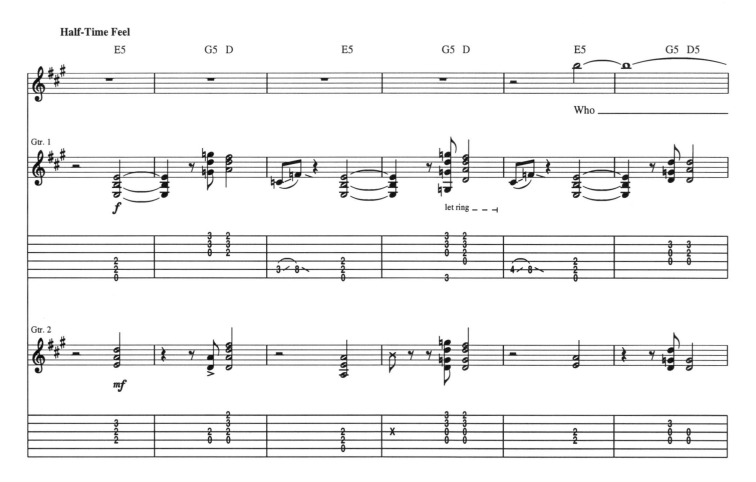

*Symbol represents chord name respective to capoed gtr.
Symbol above reflects actual sounding chord.

140

Additional Lyrics

2. I took the tube back out of town, back to the rolling pin.
   I felt a little like a dying hound with a streak of "Rin Tin Tin".
   I stretched back and I hiccupped, and looked back on my busy day.
   Eleven hours in the tin pan, God, there's got to be another way.

3. I know there's a place you walked where love falls from the trees.
   My heart is like a broken cup, I only feel right on my knees.
   I spill out like a sewer hole and still receive your kiss.
   How can I measure up to anyone now, after such a love as this?

Won't Get Fooled Again

Words and Music by Peter Townshend

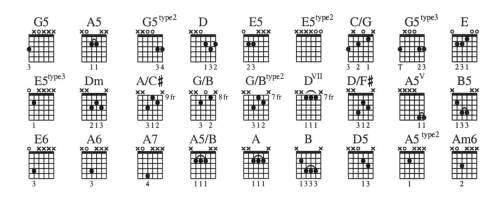

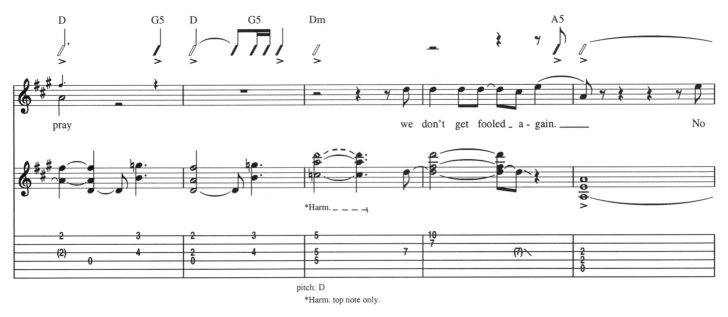

pray

we don't get fooled _ a - gain. _____ No

pitch: D
*Harm. top note only.

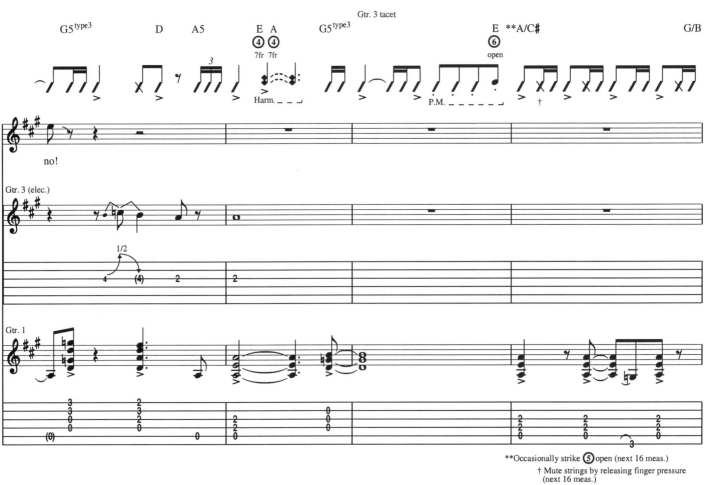

no!

Gtr. 3 (elec.)

Gtr. 1

**Occasionally strike ⑤ open (next 16 meas.)
† Mute strings by releasing finger pressure
(next 16 meas.)

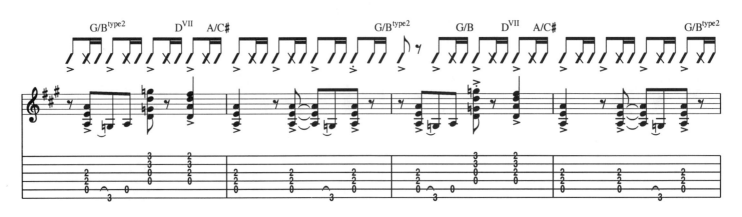

slo - gans are re - placed __ by __ the by. __ And the

part - ing on the left __ is now part - ing on the right, __ and the

* Played ahead of the beat.

Interlude

†Vibrato achieved by applying force with right hand on gtr. body & left hand on neck.

Gtrs. 1 & 2 tacet

Outro

Yeah! _____ Meet the new _ boss.

Gtrs. 1 & 3

You Better You Bet

Words and Music by Peter Townshend

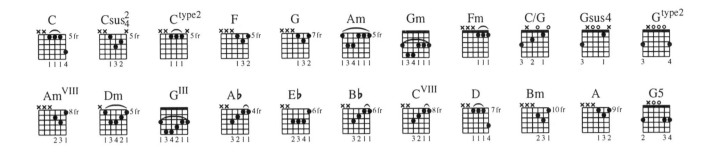

Gtr. 1: w/ Rhy. Fig. 1, 3 times, simile
Gtr. 2: w/ Rhy. Fig. 1A, 3 times, simile
(C5)

(Fsus2)

1.,2. 3.
Gtr. 2 tacet
(G) (G)

_____) (You bet-ter, you bet-ter, you bet.) (Ooh. ___ _____

%. *Verse
C
Rhy. Fig. 2

Csus$^2_4$ C^{type2} F G

End Rhy. Fig. 2

Gtr. 3
(clean)

**Bkgd. Voc. Fig. 1

End Bkgd. Voc. Fig. 1

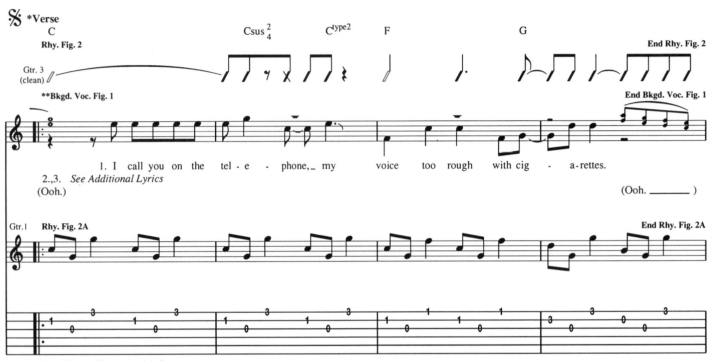

1. I call you on the tel-e-phone, my voice too rough with cig-a-rettes.

2.,3. *See Additional Lyrics*
(Ooh.)

(Ooh. _____)

Gtr.1 Rhy. Fig. 2A

End Rhy. Fig. 2A

*2nd & 3rd Verses: All parts played simile
** refers to cue-size notes only

Gtr. 3: w/ Rhy. Fig. 2, 2 times
Gtr. 1: w/ Rhy. Fig. 2A, 2 times
w/ Bkgd. Voc. Fig. 1, 2 times
C

Csus$^2_4$ C^{type2} F G

I some-times feel I should just ___ go home. but I'm deal - in' with a mem-o - ry that nev - er for - gets. _

C

Csus$^2_4$ C^{type2} F G

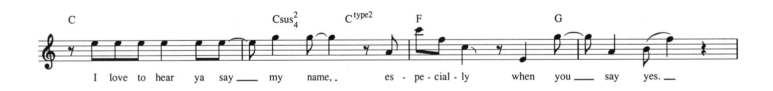

I love to hear ya say ___ my name, _ es - pe - cial-ly when you ___ say yes. _

Gtr. 2: w/ Rhy. Fig. 2, 1st 2 meas. only
Gtr. 1: w/ Rhy. Fig. 2A, 1st 2 meas. only
w/ Bkgd. Voc. Fig. 1, 1st 3 meas. only
C

Csus$^2_4$ C^{type2} F G

(cont. in notation)

Gtr. 1

I got your bod - y right now on my mind _ but I drank _ my-self blind _ to the sound of old _ T. Rex. _

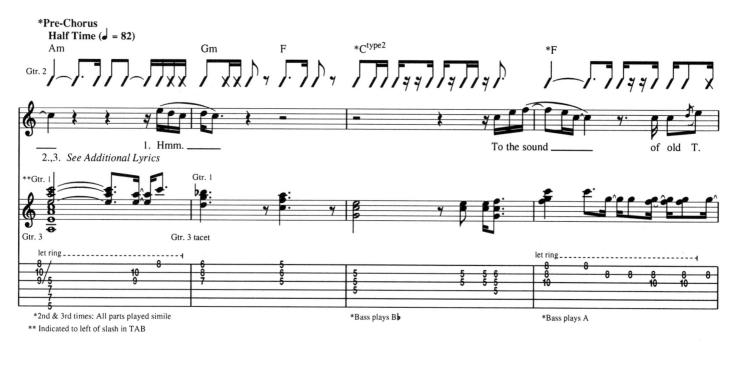

*2nd & 3rd times: All parts played simile

** Indicated to left of slash in TAB

*Bass plays B♭

*Bass plays A

*Bass plays A♭

*1st & 2nd times only

When I say I need ___ you, you say, "You bet-ter."
(Ooh. _____)

(You bet-ter, you bet-ter you

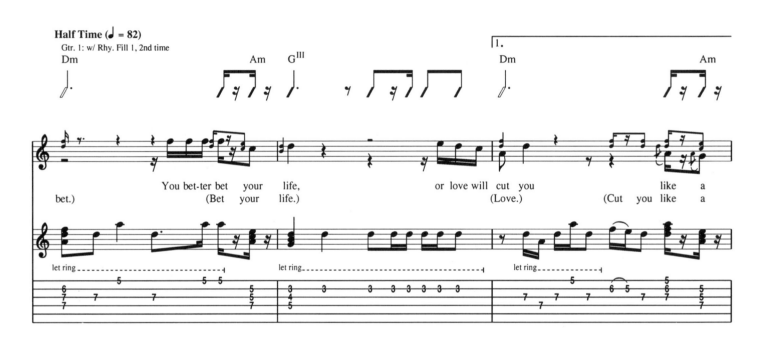

Half Time (♩ = 82)

bet.)   You bet-ter bet your life,   or love will cut you   like a
(Bet your life.)   (Love.)   (Cut you like a

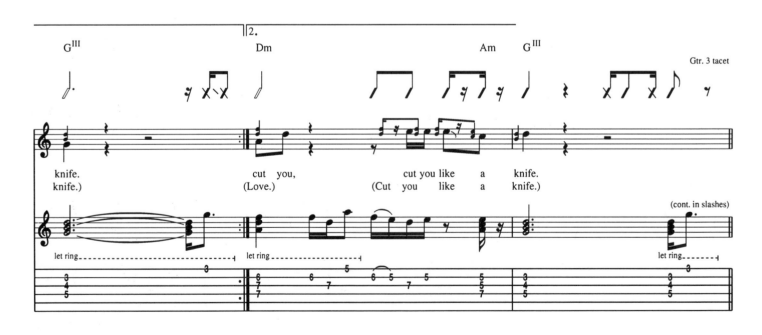

knife.   cut you,   cut you like a knife.
knife.)   (Love.)   (Cut you like a knife.)

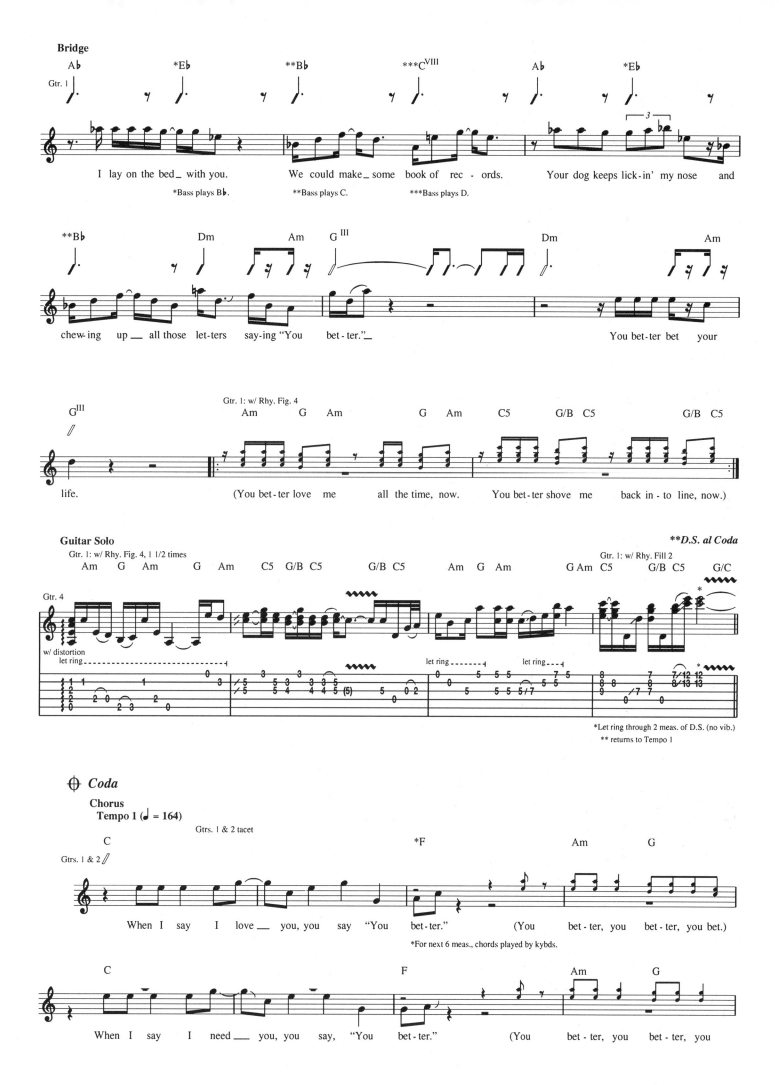

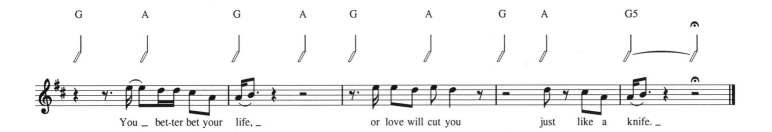

You _ bet-ter bet your life, _   or love will cut you   just like a knife. _

Additional Lyrics

Verse

2. I want those feeble-minded axes overthrown.
   I'm not into your passport picture, I just like your nose.
   You welcome me with open arms and open legs.
   I know only fools have needs, but this one never begs.

Pre-Chorus

2. I don't really mind how much you love me.
   Ooh, a little is alright
   When you say, "Come over and spend the night."
   Tonight, tonight. *(To Chorus)*

Verse

3. I showed up late one night with a neon light for a visa.
   But knowing I'm so eager to fight can't make letting me in any easier.
   I know I been wearin' crazy clothes and I look pretty crappy sometimes
   But my body feels so good and I still sing a razor line every time.

Pre-Chorus

3. And when it comes to all night living,
   I know what I'm giving.
   I've got it all down to a tee
   And it's free. *(To Chorus)*

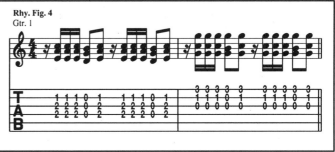

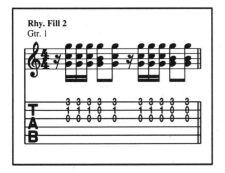

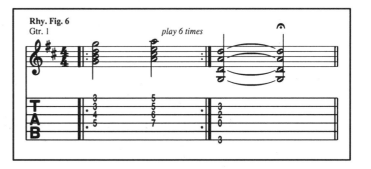

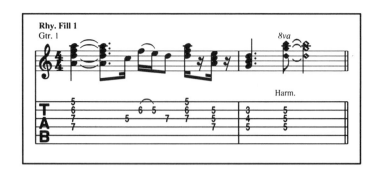

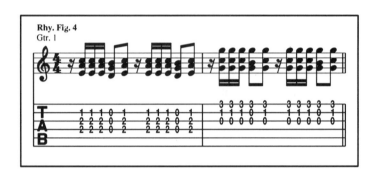

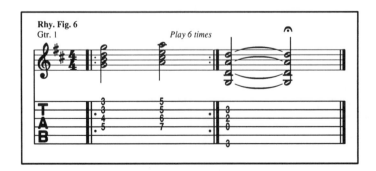

Guitar Notation Legend

Guitar Music can be notated three different ways: on a *musical staff*, in *tablature*, and in *rhythm slashes*.

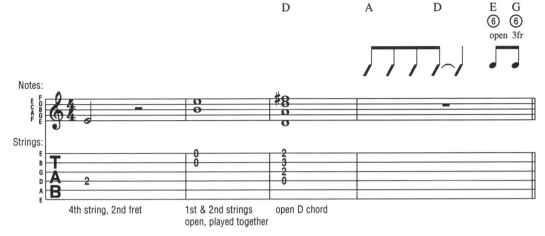

RHYTHM SLASHES are written above the staff. Strum chords in the rhythm indicated. Use the chord diagrams found at the top of the first page of the transcription for the appropriate chord voicings. Round noteheads indicate single notes.

THE MUSICAL STAFF shows pitches and rhythms and is divided by bar lines into measures. Pitches are named after the first seven letters of the alphabet.

TABLATURE graphically represents the guitar fingerboard. Each horizontal line represents a a string, and each number represents a fret.

Definitions for Special Guitar Notation

HALF-STEP BEND: Strike the note and bend up 1/2 step.

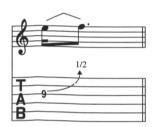

WHOLE-STEP BEND: Strike the note and bend up one step.

GRACE NOTE BEND: Strike the note and bend up as indicated. The first note does not take up any time.

SLIGHT (MICROTONE) BEND: Strike the note and bend up 1/4 step.

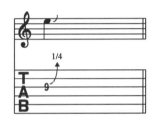

BEND AND RELEASE: Strike the note and bend up as indicated, then release back to the original note. Only the first note is struck.

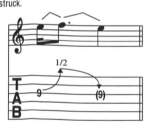

PRE-BEND: Bend the note as indicated, then strike it.

PRE-BEND AND RELEASE: Bend the note as indicated. Strike it and release the bend back to the original note.

UNISON BEND: Strike the two notes simultaneously and bend the lower note up to the pitch of the higher.

VIBRATO: The string is vibrated by rapidly bending and releasing the note with the fretting hand.

WIDE VIBRATO: The pitch is varied to a greater degree by vibrating with the fretting hand.

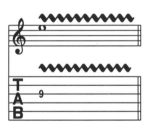

HAMMER-ON: Strike the first (lower) note with one finger, then sound the higher note (on the same string) with another finger by fretting it without picking.

PULL-OFF: Place both fingers on the notes to be sounded. Strike the first note and without picking, pull the finger off to sound the second (lower) note.

LEGATO SLIDE: Strike the first note and then slide the same fret-hand finger up or down to the second note. The second note is not struck.

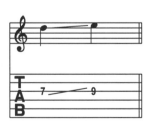

SHIFT SLIDE: Same as legato slide, except the second note is struck.

TRILL: Very rapidly alternate between the notes indicated by continuously hammering on and pulling off.

TAPPING: Hammer ("tap") the fret indicated with the pick-hand index or middle finger and pull off to the note fretted by the fret hand.

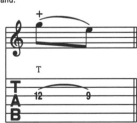

NATURAL HARMONIC: Strike the note while the fret-hand lightly touches the string directly over the fret indicated.

PINCH HARMONIC: The note is fretted normally and a harmonic is produced by adding the edge of the thumb or the tip of the index finger of the pick hand to the normal pick attack.

HARP HARMONIC: The note is fretted normally and a harmonic is produced by gently resting the pick hand's index finger directly above the indicated fret (in parentheses) while the pick hand's thumb or pick assists by plucking the appropriate string.

PICK SCRAPE: The edge of the pick is rubbed down (or up) the string, producing a scratchy sound.

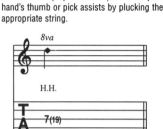

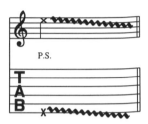

MUFFLED STRINGS: A percussive sound is produced by laying the fret hand across the string(s) without depressing, and striking them with the pick hand.

PALM MUTING: The note is partially muted by the pick hand lightly touching the string(s) just before the bridge.

RAKE: Drag the pick across the strings indicated with a single motion.

TREMOLO PICKING: The note is picked as rapidly and continuously as possible.

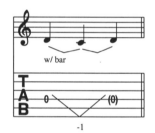

ARPEGGIATE: Play the notes of the chord indicated by quickly rolling them from bottom to top.

VIBRATO BAR DIVE AND RETURN: The pitch of the note or chord is dropped a specified number of steps (in rhythm) then returned to the original pitch.

VIBRATO BAR SCOOP: Depress the bar just before striking the note, then quickly release the bar.

VIBRATO BAR DIP: Strike the note and then immediately drop a specified number of steps, then release back to the original pitch.

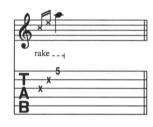

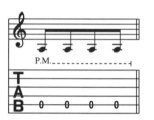

Additional Musical Definitions

(accent)   • Accentuate note (play it louder)

(accent)   • Accentuate note with great intensity

(staccato)   • Play the note short

⊓   • Downstroke

∨   • Upstroke

D.S. al Coda   • Go back to the sign (𝄋), then play until the measure marked "**To Coda**," then skip to the section labelled "**Coda**."

D.S. al Fine   • Go back to the beginning of the song and play until the measure marked "**Fine**" (end).

Rhy. Fig.   • Label used to recall a recurring accompaniment pattern (usually chordal).

Riff   • Label used to recall composed, melodic lines (usually single notes) which recur.

Fill   • Label used to identify a brief melodic figure which is to be inserted into the arrangement.

Rhy. Fill   • A chordal version of a Fill.

tacet   • Instrument is silent (drops out).

• Repeat measures between signs.

• When a repeated section has different endings, play the first ending only the first time and the second ending only the second time.

NOTE: Tablature numbers in parentheses mean:
1. The note is being sustained over a system (note in standard notation is tied), or
2. The note is sustained, but a new articulation (such as a hammer-on, pull-off, slide or vibrato begins, or
3. The note is a barely audible "ghost" note (note in standard notation is also in parentheses).